RELATE WITH ME

A Godly perspective on relationships

By Ngozi Emele

Published by
Filament Publishing Ltd
16 Croydon Road, Beddington, Croydon,
Surrey, CR0 4PA, United Kingdom.
www.filamentpublishing.com
Telephone: +44 (0)208 688 2598

Relate With Me by Ngozi Emele
© 2018 Ngozi Emele
ISBN 978-1-912256-83-9
Printed by IngramSpark

Ngozi Emele has asserted the right under the Copyright, Designs and Patents Act 1988 to be identified as the author of this work.

All rights reserved.
No part of this book may be reproduced in any way without the prior written permission from the publishers.

CONTENTS

Relate With Me: As a Book and Company	4
About The Author	5
Preface	7
Introduction	9
Section one: Singlehood	11
How can I prepare myself for the future as a single person?	15
Guidelines on how to move on	25
How to behave on your first date	31
7 tips to achieve a cheap and quality wedding	35
Section two: Marriage	41
Reasons people go into marriage	49
Keeping the fire burning in marriage	85
Section three: Babies	91
Children	99
Family	115
Conclusion	125
References/Recommendations	127

RELATE WITH ME: AS A BOOK

Relationships are a vital part our lives, and we continuously need ideas on how to sustain it. Therefore, the book serves as a guide to anyone who desires to have a good relationship either as a single person, dating, married or family, including tips on how to take care of your children.

Relate With Me was chosen as the title because the book explains diverse stages of life from a Christian perspective ranging from:

- Singlehood
- Wedding
- Marriage
- Babies and tips on how to give birth
- Parenthood
- How to support children and children in need
- How to take care of your family.

AS A COMPANY

Ngozi Emele is a writer, Christian and a lover of God. She is the director of 'Relate With Me' - a company that deals with social works activities and public health. Therefore, Relate With Me aims at continuous improvement on relationships, family and well-being. These events range from topics that deal with being single, married, dating, family, children, children in need and elderly.

ABOUT THE AUTHOR

Career
She lives in Aberdeen where she studied MSc. in Purchasing and Supply Chain at Robert Gordon University. However, she has over six years' experience working in the social healthcare sector in the United Kingdom.

Family
Ngozi is happily married to a loving husband. The couple has three lovely kids; Michelle, Hillary and Jesse.

The story of the birth of Jesse is in this book, which will give you an idea of God's faithfulness in Ngozi's life and tips on how to give birth on your own when found in a tight corner.

PREFACE

The potential for conflict in relationships arises when it involves women and men 90% of the time. Both male and female are complicated on their own. A man gets along well with men, and a woman gets along well with their fellow women, but when there is a combination of both genders, it becomes the hassle. Ignorance is the issue male and female face in relationships, and so we experiment. And while we are testing, we make mistakes and issues come up because we are not sure on how to handle our relationships. To maintain a long-lasting relationship is a significant challenge, thus the reason couples face problems. Also, it is easier to achieve a good bond if the men and women will tell each other how to love them or manage their excesses. Couples usually do not have the vital information needed to help their union survive the test of time.

There are two kinds of couples in marriages:

- Those that make it to the end
- Those that do not make it to the end

The significant difference between these two is that the former took out time to emotionally get connected to their spouse; they are passionate and happy about each other through conscious effort, word of God, prayers. It is uncommon to find couples that make it to the end on their own except by God's mercy. Just like you go to university and get trained to become a doctor or nurse, there is need to master your relationship to keep it healthy and for couples to make it to the end. The question is how do you keep yourself relevant in your home?

Being 'relevant' in your home is one way to sustain your marriage, but you have to be relevant in a way your spouse will appreciate you; this is peculiar to a couple. You will be pertinent to your spouse by learning what will keep you relevant in his or her life. For example, some men love women that dress well; if that will keep you consistent in your long-term relationship, do it.

This book will give you an insight on how best to sustain your long-term relationship (home). After reading, you must imbibe this attributes and prayerful work towards achieving relevance or successful marriage. Couples focus on their issues without sitting for a bit to identify what caused the problem they are currently facing. Was it anger? Cheating? Lies? Identifying the causes of the crisis in your home will not only help sustain your marriage, but it will give you the information or knowledge you need not to make such a mistake again.

Most of my beliefs are originated from Christ perception about marriage because a good Christian marriage is relevant to God's Kingdom and the society. Your purpose in marriage or relationship is a significant drive to its success; do you want to build a home that people or the nation will emulate? Do you want to create a relationship your friends will see and admire?

A 'good marriage' is a choice which works through a continuous effort to get better by praying to God. It's a conscious effort; it's not magic or automatic. You need to work it out yourself in agreement with your spouse, hence the word marriage is not the issue; it's us (you and me).

Dr Corey Allan, in his book *Naked Marriage*, is of the opinion that life is a choice (so is marriage).

Therefore, I choose to:

- #Grow deeper Spiritually
- #Keep it simple
- #Be passionate
- #Live in community with others
- #Enjoy the ride.

INTRODUCTION

I started blogging about relationships, and it took most of my time. I spent time writing and posting on social media with the aim to help others without realising how my husband felt.

I thought he understands and does not mind, but he is human.

I spent less time with him and more time working. It wasn't easy for me as well because I was on my maternity leave with three kids.

His behaviour changed as he gave me less support and I felt that he didn't mean well for me, my career and the business.

I became frustrated, and we started having problems.

One fateful day, I made a prayer and re-invited Jesus into my home and made him the head of my relationship officially.

He stepped in and started showing ideas on:

- When to speak
- How to speak without being misunderstood
- How to balance my work and career
- The best time to pray
- The power of positivity
- The kind of topics I should write about and discuss
- How to build a personal relationship with Jesus by reading the Bible, worshipping and fellowshipping with brethren

When I started obeying God's directives, my life, and the relationships with my husband, family and friends, became much better.

Therefore, identifying the root of your problems is key to resolving the issue. We continuously worked on the primary cause of the problem with the help of the Holy Spirit, and we achieved our desired result, which is permanent love and peace.

You too can achieve the same result by applying the above tips, which is first to invite Jesus into your life and relationship.

SECTION ONE
SINGLEHOOD

People go into relationships for different reasons. It's a choice, but you must be aware of the consequences that come with whatever decision you make. For example, if you decide to date someone sixteen years younger than yourself, you should expect some childish behaviour and attributes which may not be pleasant, while enjoying the fun that comes with dating a younger person, making you feel young as well.

Best approach to handle pressure to get married

- Are you under pressure from family and friends to get married?
- Do you feel down because people think you are getting too old and not married yet?
- Are your friends and relatives worried that you don't have a date?

Sometimes family and friends mean well for you but it's unfortunate that they go about it in a wrong way. It's not a bad idea asking your sister or brother when he or she is getting married. However, bringing up the topic now and then can be disturbing. Have you imagined yourself in their shoes? How would you react if someone keeps telling you about a particular thing you don't have at the moment? Food for thought! To be honest, everyone's life is different and so is our relationship and timing of marriage. Marrying at an early age might work for 'Miss A' whereas marriage for 'Miss B' might be later. The bottom line is that they both got married. I know that there are advantages of early marriage, but you can not marry yourself. Some people say 'I am not yet ready to get married' and I wonder why? This phrase 'am not ready' are coming from those that are ready financially, career-wise and in age, and I wonder if they are honest. I found out that some of these people are willing and they use that phrase 'am not ready' because they do not want to be under pressure.

Whether you are a Christian or not, there is power in your tongue (Proverbs 18:21) and whatever you say to yourself comes to pass; if not immediately, it will manifest in the long run. You cannot keep telling everyone around that you are not ready for marriage and go into your closure to pray to God for a spouse. On the other hand, I will not blame any single person who tells people that they are not ready. See suggested tips that will enable you to manage pressure from folks.

Advice on how to handle pressure from family and friends:

Avoid discussing so much about it unless you raised the topic.

Be open to those that have your interest at heart because some friends or family members might be able to introduce you to somebody that might be of interest to you.

Don't be shy to ask them to hook you up with someone if you want.

Pray about it daily. I talk about prayers because it's the key to everything (1 John 5:14).

Associate with others because a man or woman cannot find you when you do not make time to hang out with friends, family or colleagues. For example, church activities, workplace dinner, and any other favourable environment. "Remember where you meet your future spouse matters".

Be happy when people ask you "Are you married?" I know it's hard but the reason I say that is because some people are out to see you feel bad. Just smile and reply, "Soon," whether you are in a relationship or not. The more you confess "Soon," the quicker it comes. Be positive about it. Can you also put the question back to the person by saying, "And you? What's happening in your home or relationship?" The attention automatically diverts you to the individual.

Start planning for your future. What you don't see, you won't attract. Having a positive mindset is the key to achieving higher height in life. How many children do you desire to have (create names for them)? Start praying for your future husband or wife and children so that when you finally tie the knot, it becomes easier for you.

Work on yourself: The waiting time is a period to work on yourself. Your career, behaviour, cooking skills, and every other aspect which I may not have mentioned.

Do not focus on your past relationship. Learn to move on from your past. Focusing on your history might have a considerable influence on your behaviour towards anyone that comes around. Don't make your heart desire extreme; I know we have our taste and features we love. I reckon a partner that has 60% of what you require is okay. If you find someone that has all the attributes, great! Go for it. Just tell God the kind of man or woman you desire, and I know he will give it to you. However, he knows the beginning and the end. He can choose to provide you with another.

Leave your heart open. I am not saying you should flirt around but don't restrict yourself. For example, I must marry a lawyer or fair-skinned man. Your God-made spouse can be an engineer or some other profession which you may not fancy. Be flexible but don't go for anybody.

There is no argument on the fact that a broken relationship is better than a violated marriage. Many married couples want out of their marriage because they failed to prepare before they got married. So now is the best time to set things right because you are not married; meaning that you have an opportunity to plan yourself and tell God exactly what you want as well as position yourself for success in marriage for the future. It's not a time to cry over an ex who doesn't deserve you or cry over people who are laughing at you that you are not married. Being single is not the end of the world, it is just a phase - It's a PREPARATION TIME. Time to make things right, time to fix habits and attributes which you might not be favourable in your future home.

Seven benefits of being single (preparation time)

Single in this context means those that are not in a relationship at all. People that are single tend to be under pressure to get married especially in some parts of Africa. You will find out that your parents and friends will complain that you have reached the age of marriage and should be in your husband's house. Some people feel that you are incomplete without being married. I can understand where that perception came from which just means that the society respects you because you are married. This opinion may not be open in the mouth of many in the western world but may be in people's mind. The society does not frown at you if you have decided not to marry. It is an individual decision. Most people will want to be in a relationship or married; at least, your mind needs to be occupied by someone emotionally, which is okay and helps to keep you going. That is, if you get into the right relationship. I am not encouraging you to be alone, but my perception is that you should not spend so much time counting your age and worrying about your status.

A man or woman will find you quickly when you are busy than when you are idle. You should focus more on continuously improving your life:

- Financially
- Materially
- Spiritually
- Behaviourally
- Emotionally/psychologically
- Other

You might think the above is easier said than done. However, try to achieve the above list to an extent pending on when you meet Mr Right or Miss Right. You will appreciate my views later in life.

How can I prepare myself for the future as a single person?

1. Career

What are you doing during the preparation period?
You need to spend more time improving your job, work hard, learn new skills/further your education. Going higher and making yourself financially secure are what you should focus on more when you are single while waiting for the right person to come along. You can use this period to get a job, save up and plan for the future so that your future spouse will be comfortable. Start some investment if you can afford it. That makes life easier for yourself and unborn children. Honestly, no man or woman will want to marry you when you don't have a job or prospect of getting one. If you have finished your education to a satisfactory level, you could learn a trade or improve your God-given talent. Better still, involve yourself in the things of God by participating in church activities.

2. Spiritual

Marriage might not be so rosy always, and this is the reason I think you should equip yourself spiritually by praying and listening to the word of God via reading the Bible and fellowshipping with others in the church. Build up your relationship with God before you get married because that will help you in your trying times. Marriage comes with challenges and being close to God goes a long way to help. You will not understand what I mean until you get there. Unfortunately, we don't consider that before going into our homes. Love is beautiful, but it's not enough to sustain a household. For example, a woman could design the kind of in-laws you want through prayers.

3. Behaviour

Working on your attitude is one of the aspects to check while waiting for Mr Right. Your action is who you are at home and around the person that lives with you. Continuously working on those little habits that might eat deep into your relationship is one thing you should be doing when you are single. If you don't know your behaviour or your wrong side, you can ask your close family member, friends and your previous relationships (your exes, if you have any).

4. Search

You have enough time to find the right person but do not be choosy as it's difficult to see a perfect person. If it is possible, try and locate the right person on time, so that you can get organised regarding marriage and having babies if you want.

5. Emotionally/Psychologically

Make sure you are emotionally ready to get into a new relationship. If you are still worrying about your ex, then you might be unfit or emotionally unstable for a new relationship. Being single will help you deal with your past mindset and get you ready for your future relationship.

6. Physically

Getting ready physically involves making out time to work on your physique and appearance. If you think you are slightly overweight, that might be the reason you are still single. The preparation time will enable you to shed up any unnecessary weight by going on a diet and adopting a healthy lifestyle.

7. Travel

You have all the time to go anywhere of your choice when you are single. As soon as you get married, you need to consider your spouse, children and family needs before you can venture on any trip. Your decision is dependent on what is suitable for your spouse and children depending on their age and status. It's a good thing to be married with a family, but it comes with great responsibility. You should be willing to give up your desires most times for the family unless agreed by yourself and your partner.

8. Otherwise

Any aspect of your life which you know is not nice falls under this category. Do not change your personality entirely but don't be too extreme. Remember, too much of everything is terrible.

Disadvantages of being single

Family and friends might put you under pressure. Also, you might not attain to some positions in life if you are not married or still alone (especially in collectivist culture). There is an indirect attachment of your marital status in most things you might want to achieve in the society. Not all countries practice this. However, people see you as more responsible if you are in a relationship, engaged or married. The advantage of being single is that it will give you room to prepare yourself for the future. It is not a time to get angry but a period to get yourself ready, hence prepare yourself but don't let it take longer than necessary. Ultimately, seek to understand your future spouse because that will help you avoid experimenting in your marriage. How can I know if a guy loves me? Is it through his body expression, words of mouth or gifts?

    Sometimes, it is difficult to know when a guy loves you or not because we perceive love in diverse ways. The way you understand love and want to be loved might be different from the woman next door. Some men express their appreciation through word of mouth, gifts, kind gesture, whereas some men show their love if they have sexual intimacy with you. I believe that a guy should use words of mouth, gifts and gestures to express his appreciation to his woman. Women perceive and see things differently from men including love. The perception of life affects the way a man/woman react to his or her emotions and feelings. For example, women tend to love foreplay while making love more than men. Don't get me wrong, men love foreplay, but he will not be satisfied until he ejaculates, whereas, a woman might feel comfortable sometimes after foreplay.

Some women feel that you don't love them until you make love to them, whereas another woman gets offended if you ask her to make love to you. She feels that if you genuinely love her, you should wait until you umarry which is the right action to take. The Bible records that marriage is honourable bed undefiled (Hebrews 13:4). Also, the law of morals/society does not encourage pre-marital sex, but the community will not condemn you if you have sex before marriage.

The reason sexual intimacy happens in secret is that it's not an affair for everyone, it is an affair for married couples but the world of today has thrown all caution to the winds. My prayer is that the parents/society through the word of God should redirect our young children and youths on the right path in Jesus' name, Amen. Some men are dodgy, and they hide their personality for a long time. Furthermore, some men pretend to be who they are not and deceive women. On the other hand, we still have good men around the world. I believe that every young single woman should be able to pray and ask God for direction before going into a relationship with any man, as said in Proverbs 3:5-6:

'Trust in the LORD with all thine heart, and lean not unto thine own understanding. In all thy ways acknowledge him, and he shall direct thy paths'.

God will lead you to the person that will make you happy and love you genuinely in future as long as you ask him. For this topic, we will explain how you can tell if a guy loves you.

1. **Biblical text (1 Corinthians 13:4-7)**

'Love is patient, love is kind, love is not envious, it is not boastful, it is not puffed up. It does not dishonour others; it is not self-seeking, it is not easily angered, it keeps no record of wrongs, Love does not delight in evil but rejoices with the truth. It always protects, always trusts hopes, and always perseveres'.

From the above scripture, you know that a guy loves you if he can exhibit the high attributes towards you.

2. Also, we will look at love from a general perspective which states that a guy loves you if he:

- always wants to spend time with you;
- calls you often;
- is ready to give to you if he has;
- is interested in your well-being and career;
- intends to make you happy;
- does not struggle to tell you about himself;
- wants you to meet his family and friends;
- says he loves you;
- makes you the number one on his list of priorities;
- shows you the truth even if it hurts because he means well for you;
- is straightforward;
- does not lie to you;
- keeps you informed about his moves and updates;
- inconveniences himself to keep you comfortable;
- selflessly sacrifice;
- will be ready to pursue and support your vision, respects your opinions and choices (but can advise if he thinks otherwise about your decisions); and
- will take you down to the altar.

Please be aware that all above qualities may not be in this guy, but he should have at least 70% of them. No one is perfect including men, but you should see a high level of commitment. Having established the above statements, men should make it intentional to find out how best he can love his woman, thus learn your woman and her needs. If she wants you to tell her beautiful words, kindly do. If she loves gifts, get her what you can afford; if she is understanding, she will be glad and wait for better days.

Do not love your current woman the same way you did with your ex because they are different people and have diverse needs. However, there is a general attribute women love and is transferable such as:

- Telling a woman sweet words
- Buying of gifts
- Giving them time
- Taking pictures together
- Ability to protect them
- Helping them feel comfortable, and much more.

I want to say to our women that what you give is what you get sometimes. If you show pure love to the person you are dating or in marriage, the man will not have a choice than to reciprocate unless there are underlying issues which might make the man less interested in giving back your love.

Reasons a man will break up with you

There is no best time for a break-up. The fact is that someone is going to get hurt. It doesn't matter the day, month or year unless you both were never in love with each other which is hardly the case. A broken relationship is much better than a broken marriage. It is better for a guy to leave you before marrying him and not abandoning you when you have three/four kids for him. Men can be dodgy when they are tired of a relationship. I think it is better a guy tells a woman that he is no longer interested in the relationship than for them to leave her claiming all is well. It's now up to the lady to either hang around the guy hoping for the best or to move on with her life. Hanging around a relationship that is not making any headway for me is a waste of time. The following are reasons a guy might want to break up with you.

Distance

Distance most often than not has a significant role to play in relationships. Although sometimes a relationship works better when the individuals are apart. It can help them value their company more, but I guess it depends on how long the relationship has been. Some people cannot manage a long-distance relationship whereas others might prefer it. It's a personal thing and preference.

Doesn't fancy you anymore

A guy might want to break up with you because he is no longer interested in you based on the fact that he is either fed up with your excesses or tired of your personality.

Distracted

Being distracted is another factor when there is another girl in the picture who is giving him more love or who he thinks he prefers can make him want to quit your relationship.

Too much love

Sometimes when you give a guy or show a man that you love him 100%, you might be taken for granted. Don't get me wrong, you can show love to your man, but sometimes you don't need to open up all that is in your heart towards the person. I am aware that men like to be treated like babies but hey! A little regard for yourself won't be a bad idea.

Less attention

Giving your man less attention can make him feel that you do not love him enough. Striking a balance here is the key. You don't want to make him feel less loved or be all over him in the name of love. The ideal thing to do for me is to make him know how much you love him without making yourself worthless.

Not ready for commitment

You might be in a relationship with a guy that does not want a commitment to marriage or serious relationship. He ought to be free as the bird, and he will do you a favour by breaking up with you.

Working on it

There are some attributes you need to work on as a person which the guy you are in a relationship with does not appreciate. A behaviour 'Mr A' does not appreciate might be useful for 'Mr B'. However, there are some negative personality attributes which might be a significant trigger in a relationship. For instance, stealing could be a character trait that made your ex-partner to leave you. Now that attribute or habit is something no man will appreciate. Working on those negative features will help you to get into a better relationship as well as sustain it.

Family and Friends

Friends and family sometimes have an enormous influence on a break-up or relationship. Now, this depends on the individuals involved. A guy's family and friends may not like you and can either discourage him to break up with you or encourage him to sustain your relationship. Sometimes it's good to listen to family and friends. However, there should be a limit to what they can do for you or the advice they can give you.

Can't take up responsibility

Some men are scared of the liability that comes with family. For example, a guy might break up with you because he is not ready to financially take care of you, a baby and paying bills.

Infatuation

He could be infatuated with you in the first instance. Often, we misplace 'love' for 'infatuation'. It can be difficult to tell when a man has fallen out of love with you.

Early signs of a break-up:

- When he gets angry at you quickly
- Does not do the things he used to do
- Starts lying to you
- Becomes too busy for you for no reason
- He starts making excuses
- He stands you up on a date
- He can no longer go out in public with you
- He can't look into your eyes anymore; he can't face you especially during the heart-to-heart conversations.
- When he starts hiding his phone from you
- Not making calls in front of you
- Seems uncomfortable when you're around
- When he starts nagging at you
- When he stops calling you
- When you initiate things that will move the relationship forward, then he kicks it.

Best approach to handling heartbreak

Some of the ideas are:

- Learn to be strong
- Think less of the person by occupying your mind with meaningful things
- Forgiving yourself and learning from your past mistakes

Asking your man why there is a change in his attitude is paramount because that will help you know whether to continue in that relationship or not. However, most men will not tell you if he doesn't want you anymore. His actions speak louder than words. I presume they want women to figure it out, but most women are so in love with their men that they may not accept the truth. Of course, you cannot blame any woman; it's difficult to let off a guy if you are in love with him.

Advice for women

Please don't waste your time with a man that doesn't need you in their lives. What 'Mr A' does not appreciate to you, 'Mr B' will love. I know heartbreak can be quite hard. Just imagine the guy messing around with another woman, and you are on your bed crying and have stopped work. Now who is losing? I think it is you! Kindly stand up, wear your best hairstyle, buy new kinds of stuff for yourself and get yourself ready for the next young man. You can get yourself ready by working on those little habits that you know destroyed your former relationship. Working on these small practices will help you enter into the next relationship with a proper mindset. Make sure you are ready before you go into the future relationship but let it not take too long, so you don't miss out the right person. Before you move on, find out your wrong sides from him and work hard to improve on it, so history does not repeat itself. Above all, pray before you move into any other relationship because there are many wolves in sheep's clothing out there. It's in the place of prayer that you can get the direction. Also, open your eyes which mean you should watch and be alert in choosing a new date.

Advice for the guys

Please, if you are sure you do not want a girl or a relationship anymore, kindly let the girl know. There is no need wasting any girl's time by delaying the break-up. The early break-up will enable the person to move on quickly with her life.

Guidelines on how to move on

Moving on in dating means deciding to opt out. Moving on usually occurs if one or both parties make up their mind to quit the relationship. This decision could be based on personal, family, religious or societal reasons. It can be quite challenging to move on especially if you'd been seeing each other for several years and if you loved each other. However, some folk find it easy to do. If you ever loved them, you will miss them. Missing someone is created by thoughts, thus if you don't think about the person, you don't miss them and vice versa. Trying to distract yourself from thinking or diverting your thoughts cannot fill up the space created by this person in your heart. For these thoughts to go away, you need to understand the reasons for the idea. Is it because of money, love, intimacy or even the quarrels? The question is why do you keep thinking about this person? Answering the above question will enable you to address the reason for the thought rather than trying so hard to push it away. There are four major things that you can do for yourself to help you move on.

1. Enjoy yourself

Distracting yourself with activities that you like, such as singing, watching movies, or spending time with others. When you're happy, there won't be any need to think about the person. One of the primary reasons you believe or miss someone is the feeling that you would have been happier or better off if this person was with you. From my understanding, when you enjoy yourself, you're so glad, and when you're happy, you find it easy to move on. Remembering a good time you had together always makes you feel that you would have preferred them to be here. The mistake we make is that we select just a moment of fun, without also remembering the wrong moments (maybe fights, bad habits, amongst others). Remember the good times but remember the reasons why you ended the relationship too. Analysing both good and bad moments will help you move on.

Have you thought about the possibility that this person would have continued to exhibit those negative attributes thereby causing you more pain than happiness? Have you bothered to look at the bright side of life?

Do you believe that you can meet someone better, or have you tried to focus on your hobbies or career?

If another hurt you, do not feel that you were not good enough for him or her. Dwell more on lessons drawn from the past relationship and how to improve yourself in any relevant area.

2. Prayer

I always refer to worship because I believe so much in Jesus Christ. I have achieved so much through worship. There is a quote from the Bible that I love so much:

'I can do all things through Christ that strengthens me.'
Philippians 4:13

If I rephrase that line of scripture, I can move on through Christ that strengthens me. You will be amazed at how happy your life can become by praying for strength to move on because true happiness comes from God.

3. Clear Out

There must be physical things such as pictures, items, contacts, restaurants or people that remind you of your past relationship. Clearing out involves physically doing away with anything that tells you about your past. Clearing out has to be done because you do not want to remain in contact with the person. I see folks hanging around their ex believing that it will help them but I disagree with that. Do not get me wrong, I don't encourage enmity. However, you cannot move on if you are still close to your ex. The above high statement is true if the pain in your heart is always fresh. Less contact with your ex will aid quick recovery and thus moving on becomes more natural.

4. Reduce discussion

Avoid any discussion that will focus on the person you want to put behind you. I know friends and family might pressurise you to discuss the reason for the break-up. Make sure you speak about it when you're emotionally ready. What you don't need is anyone drawing you back emotionally; but if your emotions are strong enough for the discussion, I don't see any reason for silence. However, make sure you are speaking to the right people. You know, those in your life who inspire you? Discuss these sensitive matters with them and not with individuals who will pull your spirit down.

Controlling your thoughts is the easiest way to move on from a relationship. The human mind is broad, and no one can tell what is in another's mind, hence thoughts are ideas or feeling that cannot be seen with the physical eyes but are perceived and insinuated. If you have control over your mindset, then you will be in charge of your life and everything that surrounds it. Unfortunately, we don't seem to be able to control our thoughts. Thoughts come from what we see, hear or feel. Assuming you spend the whole day watching pornographic movies, I'm sure you know where your ideas will go. However, if you spend most of your time praying and reading the word of God, then your ideas and thoughts will be positive. For example, a married man is lusting after the wife's friend but in his mind. The wife noticed that the husband likes her through his actions and comments, but each time she asked him, he denies it. So, one day, he finally confessed to her that he has been lusting after the girl but in his mind. He imagines when he sleeps with the wife's friend but has not done it physically because the girl is married. The wife forgave him and prayed such thoughts do not occur again. Honestly seeing someone and admiring the person is not bad at all but a scenario where you keep thinking of the person and creating your world together in your mind becomes an issue.

Going by the above example, that man who is admiring the wife's friend did not do wrong. However, his primary mistake is that he kept thinking about the lady and making imaginations which could have resulted in something very embarrassing. His idea of telling the wife was not bad. Not all men will be that honest, but again it depends on the woman. Some women may not take that information lightly; they could confront their friend or do something nasty. From the story, the lady did well.

Most times, what you think is what you attract. If you start nursing the thought of sleeping with another man or woman who is not your partner, then you will soon begin working towards your goals, which is having sex with another. Your thoughts are going to graduate from admiration and fantasy into reality by you trying to get the attention of your crush either by hook or crook. By the time you realise yourself, you are in bed with someone that is not your partner. Having sex with another can then grow thick, making you either trapped into cheating permanently on your partner or ruining your relationship. Once your actual spouse leaves you because of your relationship with your flirt, you will notice that your feelings for your crush will diminish which makes it evident that you just wanted to tease a bit or you never really loved your crush. That's how powerful your thoughts are.

That's the reason; the Bible explains that as a man thinks in his heart so is he, which means that your real person is your thoughts. What defines you is what you feel in your heart and not what you do. When you sleep with a man or woman in your mind, just know that you have cheated. The earlier you work on the thoughts, the better for your relationship. Also, good motivational speakers encourage you to think positively about your business because your mindset can either make or mar your business.

Significant ways to control your thought or imagination:

- Control what you read: praying for the grace of God by reading the Bible and act on it.
- Identify what triggered those feelings and avoid it.
- Be careful what you watch.
- Who are your friends and what do they discuss?
- Speak to the evil thoughts as soon as they come. For example, in the above scenario, if an idea of sleeping with someone's wife or husband comes into your mind,

just shout to yourself and say he/she is married and can never have anything to do with a married man or woman.
- You would engage yourself by going to the shops or start reading something if the thoughts came because you were idle.
- You can also avoid evil ideas by sharing your thoughts with the genuine friends or family.
- You can seek advice from a spiritual leader.
- Avoid close contact with the person you admire.
- Replace the individual's thought with whoever you love.
- Do not keep your focus in the past; instead, concentrate on the present.
- You can distract yourself with music or any of your hobbies.
- Turn your thoughts into something positive rather than negative thoughts of cheating and sleeping with another.
- You can also write down your thoughts and imagination. Read it and you will confirm if it is something worth thinking or not.

Remember, the real you are what you think; guide your heart. Therefore, be careful how you feel and behave when you meet a potential spouse for the first time.

How to behave on your first date: What impression do you create in the mind of your first date?

Having to go out on a date with someone can be quite challenging because you do not know this person well and may not be aware of what pleases him or her. It's easier to be yourself, and there is no need pretending as your real colour will come out in future. However, you don't want to lose a girl or a guy by behaving in an immature and irresponsible way. In as much as you are advised to be real, don't be too exact as to jeopardise your chances of getting into a relationship. What your date might tolerate from you years later after you guys are close, he or she may not endure for the first time. The first impression matters in anything you do. For example, you go for an interview looking all tired and haggard. The employers will recruit an individual that is well composed and seem smart. To recruit the best candidate, the person should give out their best on the day and leave a lasting impression. The newly hired staff may not be as intelligent as the previously haggard and unserious interviewed but who cares? The first idea the interviewers got was not good enough for the role.

'Love' sometimes comes by what you see; you need swags sometimes to get your date into a relationship. It's not pretence; I call it packaging. Do not embarrass yourself in the name of trying to be real. It does not add up. You have to be physically attracted to your date first before you guys can talk or book for a time, so don't ruin it with undesirable behaviour. More so, maybe he is trying the girl's patience. However, the first impression matters. Accept the guy for a relationship if you love him. What I think is pretty good is for the man to be himself on the first date. It's either the girl accepts him or not. If he is annoying her, then it will be difficult for them to cope in the long run.

What to do before going on a date:

- Plan for it.
- Check if it's convenient for both parties.
- Look for an affordable location.
- Take time off from work.
- Make sure you are sound, emotionally and health-wise.
- Rehearse your responses or talks, if possible.
- Dress to kill.
- Don't book it if you cannot afford.
- Be confident in doing something that makes you feel relaxed. For example, for women, getting your nails done.
- Don't come with a negative attitude from your past or stories; stay positive.
- Be happy and let your personality shine through. Get a friend to come hang over before you go on a date or go from a friend's house because that might help remove any form of fears or nervousness.
- Look up your first on social media, just to get a idea of their personality. You might get to know things that they fancy or not. Do not let them know you did that; it's just to satisfy curiosity.
- Be advised not to confuse the information you get with them on social media and what they told you during the first.
- Be patient enough to understand them first before judging them.
- To boost your self-esteem, you can exercise, play music and think about the things you like about yourself a few hours before your date.

What to do on your first date:

- Make it memorable.
- Make sure you save up some money.
- Be as real as possible but don't showcase your bad sides.
- Be ready to listen to the other party, don't just keep talking and talking. Take a moment and learn about this person by asking questions.

- Avoid talking about your past relationships or dates unless your date asks you. That discussion can come up later.
- Build it on honesty and don't tell lies which might come back to haunt you later in the relationship.

Advice for women:

- If you love a man, you will overlook his excesses.
- Do not go into a relationship with the mindset you can change a person because you might not.
- Any man that can't share a penny with you today will not share millions with you tomorrow.
- Discuss any issues you notice.
- Some men exhibit some attitude to test your patience; be patient enough to understand what is going on. If it occurs again and again, then it doesn't worth it.
- Dress well.
- Make sure your care is spot on.
- Look neat.
- Pay attention to the chemistry between the two of you, don't get overexcited or infatuated. Make sure your reactions are mutual so it doesn't look like your falling head over heels whereas he may not call you back.
- Let yourself go and have fun, don't be too uptight. This tip might be for the women that are an introvert. Don't bore the guy by being too quiet.

Advice for men:

- Learn to share the little you have with your first date.
- No woman likes to hang around a stingy man.
- Do not swear as you do not know if your date is offended by swearing or not.
- Carry yourself like a gentleman just for that day. It's not pretence.
- You don't have to show that you're the man, your actions will speak for you, like paying for the meal.

- Listen to the woman when she talks.
- Look into her eyes as well, i.e. make intimate eye contact with her.

When you have accepted to marry your date, you need to arrange a wedding. Planning for a quality wedding involves time.

7 tips to achieve a cheap and quality wedding

Many people focus more on how big their wedding party can be without actually thinking about the lifetime commitment. Some tend to borrow from friends and family or, better still, from banks just to show off on that day. Others depend solely on either their friends, family or well-wishers to have a grand day. Don't get me wrong, I am not saying that your friends and family cannot support you financially, but you should not depend on them for all your wedding expenses. The couple-to-be should make time and organise themselves by planning according to their available funds bearing in mind that they have to save for rainy days after the wedding. Planning a wedding is not rocket science, and it doesn't take years to prepare as people think. However, this depends on how you want your wedding and what you hope to achieve. A beautiful wedding is in mind and simplicity, I believe, is the best approach to that. Below are tips that will help you enjoy the best day of your new beginning as a couple.

Praying

I gave this as a number one tip because this opens up ideas on how to go about your wedding and the right people to meet. Asking God for direction is the key to a successful marriage because it will give him room to cover the aspect you can not handle – that is the spiritual aspect. Some people/folk might not be happy that you are getting married but prayer covers you from all that jealousy, and evil intents in the hearts of some people that you might not be aware have a contrary intention towards your day or marriage in future.

Available Funds/Budget

Learning how to budget as an intending couple is a good start for the future. It does not make sense to borrow just to organise a wedding. An intending couple must learn to work with what they have because this will help them manage their funds in future.

Agreement

The Bible says that can two walk together, except they agreed? (Amos 3:3) The intending couple needs to decide on what they want: either elaborate/society wedding, secret/court marriage or marriage blessing. Most couples organise a court marriage and marriage blessing (church), but this is your choice to make.

Invited guests

Be careful the number of guests you request and make room for extra people, just in case. You don't want to run out of meals and drinks. If you can afford an elaborate wedding, then it's no problem; but if you are struggling, then you might best plan the day yourself and invite less guests.

Bridesmaids/Groomsmen

The bridesmaids and groomsmen should be able to buy their wears based on your agreement with them. That will help save you some money. Also, inform them at the time so that you don't take them unawares as everyone has got one financial commitment or the other.

Lose weight/appearance

I have heard of scenarios where people try to lose weight to fit into their wedding dress or suit. If you think you are overweight and want to shed weight for your wedding to look good, then it's not a bad idea. Weight loss is one of the most challenging tasks to handle, but I guess it needs self-discipline and determination to achieve your desired size.

Choice of wears

What you wear to your wedding has a long way to affect how people perceive your day. It's not about an expensive wedding dress, jewellery, suits, shoes. It's what fits you and partner as well as colour that matches your skin colour. I know that the right quality wears are expensive, but I also know that no matter how costly your wedding attire is, if it doesn't fit or match your skin colour, then no one is going notice if you bought it cheap or expensive. On the other hand, some brides choose not to have a wedding train. The bride and groom are just fine with the best man and maid of honour which is lovely and straightforward depending on what they want.

To conclude, if you can afford an elaborate wedding, kindly go for it, but if you can't, you have two options:

1. It's either you wait until you get financially ready which might take ages or less; in some cases, the relationship is destroyed while waiting for that big wedding, whereas it works for some people.

2. Or you go ahead and have a low-key wedding that you and partner can afford.

Bear in mind that there will always be time for anniversaries and if your financial status changes, you can still celebrate and have your desired wedding in the future. The bottom line is for us to cut our coat according to the size of our cloth. Have a right wedding if you can but please do not owe afterwards.

How to carry out a health and safety check for a wedding

Health and safety check (HSE) is paramount in anything you want to do in this life. Health and safety check just means testing how safe an environment is to you and others. It can involve many processes such as carrying out possible risk assessment and hazards perception that might occur in a particular context. For example, a couple decided to have a wedding reception on a plank which got eighty people drowned into the water underneath. A proper health and safety check was not carried out from that story. Organising a wedding is not a problem, but an awareness that humans are involved and carrying out maximum security check is essential to avoid the incident. The couple were lucky that in this scenario, no one died because that would have been more disastrous than what they experienced. The wedding organisers didn't consider the children or people with learning difficulties who may not be conscious of the environment. Putting all guests into consideration is pertinent because an older woman who was wheelchair bound was affected as well. There is no need jeopardising the lives of individuals all in the name of making your day unique. While you're planning for your wedding, please do not forget to keep everyone safe. Before planning a wedding, a risk assessment (HSE) should be carried out, meaning analysing what can cause harm to you or anyone in a particular place or location. For this scenario, we will examine a possible risk assessment for a wedding location.

It involves the following:

- Get an excellent location.
- Check if the environment is safe.
- Consider who your guests are and make necessary plans for their safety or help them access their needs such as setting up an accessible welfare facility.
- Keep everywhere safe for the children, children with disabilities, adults, vulnerable adults and older people.
- Know the number of people you are inviting and make enough room for them.
- Provide food according to your ability. Sometimes you go for a party and you realise that their meal was not sufficient because the number of the guests were more than the food made available.
- My candid advice; invite the number of people you can afford so that you can make adequate preparations to cater for them.
- Make sure kitchen utensils are clean and stored away.
- Parking spaces for adults and vulnerable adults to avoid any form of exclusion.
- Consider how many children are coming and think about

how to entertain them or how safe their playing area will be.
- Carrying out fire alarm checks.
- Identify hazards such as drink spill, banana peels, etc. and put a plan in place to cover up in case such incidents occur.
- Provision of basic First Aid kit which might be helpful if someone hurts himself before an ambulance arrives.
- Make sure the meal prepared is checked to avoid food poisoning.
- Check if your drinks are expired; you don't want people complaining of stomach ache after your occasion.

Please be careful how you organise your wedding and carefully choose your location. Be aware that it is a one-day event which I think should be memorable but you don't want it to be a negative one. You want to leave your wedding safely. While planning for a reception location such as the beach, make sure everyone is safe. Yes, there is a place for prayers, but you need to play your part by carrying out the necessary checks around.

This risk assessment refers to activity, environment and the people.

- You write the date of the evaluation.
- The signature of who conducted the risk assessment.
- Print full name of the individuals getting married.
- Write a brief description of the needs of the couple-to-be and guests, the activity or the environment assessed and why it a risk.
- Identified hazards linked to the above description. Think of how to minimise the risk.
- Food and hygiene - plates, cups, drinks, chefs, eating perishable in time are advisable and non-perishable ones served later to avoid food poisoning.
- Cutlery should be kept clean and put away after use especially knives to prevent children playing with them. They should be held away from kids as well.

Control measures to think of on the wedding day:

- There should be a disposable bin around to put dirty meals or leftovers, and that should be put away immediately outside by volunteers who have been assigned to help out on your wedding day.
- Organise people that will contribute to clean the floor from any form of water or banana peels to avoid falls of any kind.
- The announcement should go round for individuals to look out for fire exits in case of fire and the meeting point should be explained just in case but guess no one prays for such a day.
- Anyone that needs to dance can see the floor type. An announcement for everyone to be careful while dancing depending on the kind of shoe and cloth won by such individual.
- Let parents know that the care of their children is in their hands and everyone is responsible for taking care of their kids unless the couple has made adequate arrangement for kids and carers for the hours of the reception. However, some wedding planners have made it clear that children are not allowed in their dinner which for me is better to do than to provide an unsafe environment for them both environmentally, psychologically and emotionally.

You can rate the risk before and after the control measures have been put in place. It could be high, low, very high, negligible, controlled or uncontrolled. The above analysis is a rough idea of how to do a risk assessment of any environment, but it depends on the location and the people you intend to invite on your wedding day. The bottom line is for us to be careful when choosing the location of your wedding reception to avoid death or any form of injury as seen from the previous scenario. After the wedding, the marriage journey begins which ideally should be a lifetime commitment.

SECTION TWO
MARRIAGE

Marriage from my understanding is about 'growing up'. It's not rocket science and not complicated as most of us think. The easiest way to achieve what I call a 'modest marriage' includes a fervent prayer to God for grace to continuously 'mature up' on little habits that do not favour your home. These patterns or attributes may not go away quickly, but an awareness of your weaknesses is a starting point in achieving the modest marriage. Personally, I have learnt a lot from my union in the last eight years. I am still learning and will continue to learn, thus the continuous improvement which is the target of 'Relate With Me'.

Your perception or views about marriage goes a long way to affect your behaviour in it. Some people enter marriage believing that it's not a do or die affair meaning they don't mind if they separate or not. I think that's a wrong mindset. For a home to be stable, the 'it must work' ideology must be adopted. This mindset will enable you to put in your best. However, if your marriage involves issues such as domestic abuse violence, exploitation and maltreatment, then I wouldn't advise you to stay unless you have an assurance of your safety. That's my humble opinion. The importance of a good marriage in our lives and society cannot be overemphasised.

Importance of Marriage

Every individual is a product of some relationship or marriage. We came as a result of the relationship between a man and woman. Your parents may not have been married and may have been divorced. Also, you may have come out a marriage full of turmoil or peace, but the fact remains that you came into the picture because of a relationship. Marriage from my opinion is a vital part of our lives. However, some people do not value friendship especially in the world of today. These type of people think that marriage is a bondage and boring; others feel that they do not have the opportunity to explore or have extramarital affairs making them hooked with one person.

The importance of marriage is in three sections.

Importance of Marriage: as an individual

Some folk have been in a relationship with one man for close to ten years, and they are still partners which does not make any difference to me because if you can live with someone for such number of years, you might as well legalise it and tie the knot. The issue with some folk is that they are scared of the marriage or maybe they are worried that if the relationship does not work out, they might lose their properties or inheritance. You do not have anything to lose by being married because it saves you having to jump from one relationship to another and in return, you have your health intact as you will have one sexual partner. I know that some married people cheat on their spouse, hence marriage is not a guarantee to be faithful. However, the chances of cheating are low when you are married to someone you love. Again, this is a personal decision or an individualist thing. There are so many reasons why a man or woman will cheat on the spouse in their marriage.

Cheating in marriages

The fact is that anyone can cheat on the partner or spouse. Most women that cheat on their husbands are not sex-starved, thus many women trick as well as men. People cheat for different reasons. It could be for fun or due to one challenge or the other.

Possible reasons men and women cheat:

- To get happiness
- When challenges of life hit them
- Low self-esteem
- Lack of love in their relationships or homes
- No sexual satisfaction
- Retaliation
- Tired of their man
- Disappointment from their man
- Lack of trust

- Still in love with their ex-partner
- When they are in love with another
- Have not moved on from their past

There is no moral justification for cheating, and it's either the relationship is working or not. Also, it's either your working towards improving on those little habits or issues that are tearing your relationship or your functioning towards destroying it by seeking for alternatives. However, any man who can marry a woman and deny her of that critical aspect of the relationship has a problem. It's either he is not physically attracted to the woman, or he loves another. The question is "How long will the woman cheat in the marriage to maintain her home?" Let's assume the husband hasn't touched her for ten to twenty years. She will have to sleep with different men for twenty years as she may not be able to keep a man for that long outside, thus exposing herself to diseases and unhealthy relationships. Most women hang onto their marriage because of their children; great reason, I must confess. However, those children will leave home and forge ahead with their lives, making the woman unhappy for the rest of her life by sticking to her husband, hoping for a change. Changes apply to those that welcome it. The only person that can change a person's attribute is God, but you have to desire a change as well as work towards achieving it.

Tips that can help anyone in such a situation are:

- Pray about it.
- Identify the cause of the issue.
- Access the person by finding out how to take care of him in bed.
- Seek advice from a family, good friends or spiritual authority (pastor/counsellor).
- The woman should evaluate herself to see what she is not doing right.
- Ask for a divorce if the situation lingers for long and she cannot cope.

The above applies to both men and women. The woman is the point of reference for the purpose this study.

Sometimes, marriages are challenging, but these challenges are faced by the couple or either of them. Life is too short to tie oneself in such an emotional mind torture. However, there is always room for continuous improvement on the part of the man if he is willing and desires a change because no one can decide for him. 'Communication' will help both the man and woman to discuss their sex life. If the husband is not forthcoming for the discussion, the woman should meet him and initiate the conversation. There is nothing to hide from your spouse. If your husband or wife is doing something you do not appreciate during sex, just let the person know rather than abstaining from having sexual intercourse with the individual. Tell your spouse what turns you on and how best he or she can satisfy you in bed. Do it! Please be advised whatever you choose should not be to the detriment of your health.

There is a need for couples to pray together often to keep the relationship. This point applies to all relationships; holding hands together to pray is a sign of unity and goes a long way to have a positive impact on the family. God is the head of any union, marriage or relationship. I do not encourage divorce because 'Relate With Me' aims to improve on relationships and marriages continuously. However, it doesn't condemn anyone that is divorced because you can't force two adults to be together. I will offer advice and pray the relationship does not dissolve.

Importance of marriage as a Christian

The first institution in the Bible is marriage/relationship, thus the reason it is essential to Christians. As a born-again Christian that has a fear of God, you are not allowed to live with a man or woman that you are not legally and spiritually married to. The Bible frowns at it as said in Hebrews,

>'Marriage is honourable, bed undefiled'
>– Hebrews 13:4

However, our God is merciful, and he does not hold our sins against us, but we do not have to take that for granted. For your emotional needs to be met as an adult, you need to be married to enjoy the benefits of sexual intimacy and companionship. Anything you do outside the box is a sin and unfit for the kingdom of God according to the book of all books (Bible).

Therefore, the importance of marriage as a Christian:

- It helps you abstain from a sin of fornication (1 Corinthians 6:15-18).
- You will be obeying the scripture that encourages you to be fruitful and multiply by reproducing children (Genesis 1:28).
- It pleases God when you follow (Hebrews 13:4).
- Marriage is the first institution ordained and approved by God (1 John 5:18).

Importance of marriage to the community

Marriage is an agreement between two who have decided to be together. Union has a social and economic benefit to the society. Marriage in some cultures is a way of having children, thus increasing the family lineage as well as the community at large. Children are known as leaders of tomorrow. Therefore, they will help to maintain a community in future. Communities and cultures understand marriage from diverse views and preferences. In the western culture settings, a union is established by love and emotions whereas some societies, such as the collectivist culture, understand marriage as an obligation to have a family. In the collectivist culture, a woman is not recognised as complete until she marries. However, western civilisation does not have an issue whether a woman is married or not. Western culture believes in marriage, but their religion does not place single women under pressure to marry. Marriage helps to avoid societal issues such as unwanted pregnancies, sexually transmitted (AIDS), divorce, adoption, separation which hurts children, bullying, which occurs as a result of children who were not trained properly, and much more.

Understanding your spouse

Every relationship has rules that guide it. What works for 'Couple A' will not work for 'Couple B' which means something that works for 'Husband A' as a surprise might be annoying for 'Husband B'. The ability to learn what your spouse will appreciate is the key to the sustenance of your relationship. Doing something for your husband because your friend did for hers will be a bad idea because they are different individuals with diverse perceptions about life.

Significant tips on how to learn about your spouse:

- By asking questions directly or indirectly
- Learn from previous experience with your partner.
- Learn from last argument/fight.
- Ask a family member or your partner's good friend.
- By saying what you desire to do to check his or her response.
- Finding out your spouse's interests and preferences.

Tips on how to surprise your man:

Every person is different, and they behave and react differently, so it's sometimes difficult to understand or have a general knowledge of how to surprise a man. The tips that follow on how to surprise a man may not apply to all people, but from the 'Relate With Me' Facebook group discussion, the information gathered explains that men do not usually appreciate some surprises. You must have at the back of your mind that your spouse can either like the surprise or not. However, you have to be positive by believing that it will work because our mindset can have an impact on what we do, including shocks.

- A birthday gift or party depending how much it's bought the family financial status.
- Buying new nightwear to look different for them.
- Creating new sex tricks to increase intimacy and fun (important for men).

- Celebrating anniversaries.
- Wearing his favourite kind of dress.
- Changing your hairstyle the way he likes it.
- The news of pregnancy.
- Any news he has been long waiting for such as work letter, business ideas, deals etc.
- Breakfast in bed.
- Tell your partner one thing about him you love which you have never said before.
- Romantic message or text through your phone while in the same house.

The above tips depends on the mood of the man that day. Please be advised that you should not give your husband surprise when he is grumpy or has a bad week because it may not turn out well. Your ability to know when to pull a trick is quite essential to avoid hurt. Men should be able to accept anything their wife presents because it's disappointing making out time to do something and it's not appreciated. The wife may not have the urge or the mind to put up surprises with the fear that it may not be accepted. If you as a man do not like the surprise your spouse gave you, appreciate her first and then explain later on to her in a way that she will understand that you do not fancy such a surprise. She can then ask you the kind of things you like and dislike.

Best ways to tell your spouse you don't like a surprise:

- Pretend you like the surprise to avoid hurt.
- Enjoy the shock to the best of your ability.
- Tell her how you appreciate the fact that she made time to organise a surprise and you understand her.
- Look for when she is in a good mood to discuss.
- Finally, explain to her that you don't like such surprises, stating your reasons.
- Give her the best ways to surprise you and how to go about it for future purposes and encourage her to try them out.

What to do if your surprise does not work out.

- Have a discussion.
- Find out the reason your spouse does not like the surprise.
- Find out the best mood to surprise your spouse.
- Don't get so worked up or angry if he or she doesn't like your surprise.
- Accept your mistake and learn from it.
- Do not say you will never surprise him/her again.
- Work with the information you got from him or her, being aware of his or her preferences and future best approach.

Reasons people go into marriage

Money

Some people go into a relationship because the other person is financially stable. Having money sometimes can bring comfort and happiness in a relationship or marriage, so individuals prefer women or men that are financially buoyant to avoid any issues with poverty or lack. They say money is the root of all evil whereas the Bible believes money answers all things, hence the absence of money in a relationship causes a rift if not adequately managed.

Remedy - Pray: The solution to financial insolvent in relationships is firstly prayers. Praying for your economic status will help give you strength to carry on until change comes.

Affordable deals: Go for the items and products you can afford until a change comes. Yes, you want the best things in life, but you cannot provide it for now. Manage yourself and go for things that you need and not things that you want.

Right associate and friends: If you are going through financial problems, be careful who you call your friend and do not mingle with folks that make you feel sorry about your situation. Do not be jealous of anyone; however, do not let anyone put you under pressure because you do not have what they can afford. Yours will come by God's grace.

Mindset: Your mind lies issues of life. Your mindset can make or mar you. Think the right thoughts and be positive. The Bible records that you should guard your heart with all diligence because out of it are issues of life (Proverbs 4:23) and Les Brown in his video Positive Mindset states that whatever you become tomorrow starts from your mindset. What you do not desire, you can not attract. So believe in yourself and that you will make it in life but in a positive way.

Fame

If the person happens to be famous, then it's right for you: enjoy the moment, and it's a blessing, but that should not come first.

Remedy: You should have a priority of what you want in a life partner. One's status in the community is not the first on the list because that can fail you in a relationship. Your initial concerns should a spouse that fears God, hardworking, love, intelligent and much more. If the person happens to be famous, then it's right for you. Enjoy the moment, and it's a blessing, but that should come first.

Beauty

Beauty, they say, is in the eyes of the beholder which means that what 'Individual A' classifies as beauty may mean being ugly in the eyes of 'Individual B'. A man can go into a relationship or a date with a woman just because of how beautiful she is. Again, that is understandable because we all have our preferences in life.

Remedy: Yes, you should go for the physical appearance or beauty of someone, but the beauty is the inward one. If a woman is beautiful and does not have a good behaviour, her natural vision is going to fade away in no distant time. So inward grace is more important (1 Peter 3:3). Also, if a beautiful lady comes for an interview well-dressed and the interviewee seems pleased to behold such a beauty, but when the conversation starts, and she doesn't deliver, that vision will fade away, and there is a high tendency that she will not get the job, hence inward grace outweighs outward beauty anytime, any day.

Family

Someone's family background can sometimes determine the kind of person one dates or marries. A woman could say "I heard that family are lovely people, hence I would love to be in a relationship with a man from that family."

Remedy: All that glitters is not gold. Prayerfully and watchfully choose where you end up in marriage because that determines how far you will go in life. A genuine God-fearing family makes love and care is a essential part of their lives. However, it doesn't mean challenges might occur in the cause of the marriage.

Hardworking

No one will want to go into a relationship with a lazy person. Everyone wants a man or woman who is willing to work and make ends meet instead of sitting and spending without earning. The level of wealth sometimes can determine your needs to work or not, but on a general note, most people go into a relationship just because that individual is hardworking and is willing to contribute towards any project or family needs. The Bible encourages you to study to show yourself approved which means you need to work hard to gain support. Also, the university will not award you a certificate if you don't make good grades.

   Remedy: Your gender status is not an excuse to be lazy. Whether you are a man or woman, work to improve yourself daily, academically, skills, business or whatever you find yourself doing. The rule that should guide you is 'ctrl do something' – meaning you must not be comfortable doing nothing unless for health reasons such as maternity, illness etc.

Giver

Individuals, especially women, prefer men that are willing to give and take care of them. Offering, from my views, does not apply when you have everything; a giver can share a pound from the little he or she has with his/her partner. When you are a giver, you can attract yourself a date or a good relationship.

   Remedy: Giving is an excellent attribute to imbibe because givers never lack (Acts 20: 33-38). Associating yourself with a giver brings you blessing and success, thus endeavour to be a giver. Do not depend on your spouse or the person you are dating to give on your behalf.

Love

Love is quite a broad topic, thus the reason it will take a more detailed approach, and it connects to other aspects of any relationship or marriage. Love is one of the primary reason people identify that helps them go into a relationship. You hear folk say, "I just love him, and that's why I am hanging out with him," and there must be a reason or reasons why you love or have developed feelings for this person. Love is the general word for the above attributes because you might like someone because the individual is a giver, hardworking, rich etc.

Remedy: Show love to your spouse or the person you are dating through your behaviour, word of mouth and through gifts.

Business benefit

Some people go into a relationship because of what they stand to gain from the person involved. If dating a guy can give a woman contract, sometimes this woman goes for it just to have access to the business ideas and gain. For example, when a friend that wants to coax you into sleeping with him or her before she can help connect you to a business or give you ideas, that will enable your company to exhilarate to a higher level.

Remedy: Do not marry someone because of what you will gain in business. Marriage is a lifetime commitment and business benefits aren't a strong reason to marry someone.

Religious beliefs

Religious beliefs go a long way to determine who one dates or not. It is rare to find individuals with diverse ideas coming together because their thoughts will be different and sometimes it's difficult to manage. One can choose to date or go into a relationship because he or she is a Christian or any other religious background.

Remedy: Honestly, getting married to someone you have the same belief in is essential. You may not understand it until you get involved with someone that does not believe in your God. Sometimes, people with different opinions get along well, but it depends on the individuals and how they are willing to accommodate one another's ideas and religious beliefs. However, it's easier when you live with someone that understands your religious obligation and is on the same page with you.

Ethnicity

Marrying based on ethnic is the order of the day. That's not to say that people from different ethnic background don't mingle but I think that will depend on where you live and your associations. In the western world such, as UK and USA where you have individuals from diverse ethnicity living together, you find young people dating anyone, not minding your original background or ethnicity. Some countries, especially in Africa, are keen on who you marry and where the person is from which will determine whether you will date that individual or not.

Remedy: I do not see anything wrong with marrying someone from a different culture from you. Neither am I against anyone marrying from his tribe. However, be ready to accommodate your spouse's religion because the different ways of life will come into play at some point in the relationship. All you need is wisdom and tolerance to be able to cope with it.

Bind two families

Different families want their children to marry to cement their relationship or for mutual benefits, maybe in business, friendship, or for any other reason, so the children will decide to go into a relationship just to make their parents happy and keep or maintain the long-term family relationship.

Remedy: Do not marry to cement a family relationship. No one is going to live with you in your home, hence be advised that when your family connects you and spouse, it will no longer be a family issue, it becomes your personal affair. You will have to deal with the challenges alone unless you employ the help of Holy Spirit.

Sex

Apart from love, sex is another primary aspect of marriage. It's possible for a person to marry another based on his or her tactics in bed (sexual satisfaction he or she derives from that relationship). Sex is one of the primary reason people go into a marriage.

23 reasons you should have sex daily

Sex is a very important for our health and relationship. It is a topic we should be happy to discuss as it can make or mar your relationship or life.

Reasons people shy away from discussing the topic sex:

- Religious background
- Moral
- The societal environment
- The fear of talking vulgar
- Worried about how people will see you
- It's a private affair
- Some people feel uncomfortable with the topic

Sex is one of the most critical aspects of any marriage. A union where the couple doesn't engage in lovemaking is going to break anytime soon, thus sexual intimacy between couples helps to sustain their relationship. To answer the question as to "How many times are couples allowed to have sexual intimacy?" - it's unlimited. No law states that couples should make love once or twice a day. The number of times should be unlimited, but it depends on the couple. In a relationship, it's either one party's libido is high or the other person's libido is low, but this is not always the case. The person that has the smaller impulse should try and match up with his/her partner for maximum sexual satisfaction. However, if both couples have the same level of desire, then carry on and enjoy yourselves. In a scenario where you cannot meet up with the sexual demand of your spouse, it is essential you communicate to avoid any issues.

Reasons one might not meet up with sexual demands:

- Just had a baby
- Pregnancy sometimes may pose a challenge
- Health reasons
- Fasting and prayer
- Travelling

- Busy at work
- Not in a right state of mind
- Cheating on the spouse
- Fallen out of love
- Issues with his/her libido
- There is no chemistry between the couple
- Angry at spouse

To be honest, the more sex you have, the better your health and everything around you. There is a link between your health and relationship. See the 23 reasons below.

Benefits of sexual intimacy:

- To relax your nerves
- It helps you to have a high level of concentration in your business
- Enables you to laugh more
- It helps to keep you happy, and in return, you will keep everyone around you happy
- Good for your health
- Increases intimacy
- Sexual intimacy resolves all problem or arguments
- Reduction of stress
- It's a good exercise for the body, and you can burn calories
- Helps to keep your period regular
- It brings down your blood pressure
- Sex prepares pregnant women for delivery
- Helps to maintain a healthy pelvic muscle
- It helps you to keep a healthy heart
- Lowers a man's risk of having prostate cancer
- A functional cure for a cold
- It helps increase your daily confidence
- It helps you look younger than your age sometimes
- Increase fertility if you are looking for a baby
- Reduce chances of menstrual cramps
- Reduce headaches

- It helps you sleep well, especially at night
- Helps you live a longer life

Lack of sexual intimacy can:

- destroy a relationship;
- lack of sexual intimacy hurts your mood;
- not good for the health;
- it affects your relationship negatively;
- makes you frustrated;
- low concentration of high workload;
- constant fight among the couple;
- and much more!

The importance of sexual intimacy between couples cannot be overemphasised. Increase your sexual activities in your home, and I can assure you that you will enjoy a better health and relationship between you and your spouse.

Remedy: Sexual intimacy is not right if you are not married. Apart from what the Bible says that marriage is honourable, bed undefiled (Hebrews 13:4). The law of morals does not encourage pre-marital. However, no one will condemn if you indulge in pre-marital sex, but it pays to keep yourself before marriage. Staying safe will keep you away from dangers such as diseases, abortions, unwanted pregnancies; these are among societal issues.

Leave to remain

A permit to live in a country can be challenging to get and it depends on the immigration rules that govern that country. Some people might decide to date or marry someone because they want to get their permanent residence to live in that country. Sometimes, this set of individuals tend to develop genuine feelings for each other after having lived together for a while. Please be advised that 'Leave to remain' does not apply to every relationship or all because not everyone migrated from his or her country to settle down.

Remedy: My question at this point is what happens when you get your papers? Will you divorce your spouse? Remember you must have wasted many years of your life just to achieve that and you can not gain the time back. What happens to your children if you have any? Have you thought about the effect of divorce on them?

The Bible firstly is against divorce. Jesus' wisdom in male or female relationships: Matthew 19 summarises Jesus' opinion and beliefs about marriage, divorce and relationships. During the time of Malachi, a man could divorce the wife for so many reasons. For example, if a woman was on her menstrual cycle and refused to tell the husband about it, then it becomes a problem and he can divorce him. But all that has changed, as we read in Matthew 19. Jesus does not encourage divorce except if the person has committed adultery. However, he further asked a question that anyone that has got no sin should first throw a stone at the woman. The above story means the solutions to resolving problems in relationships are not divorce, but forgiveness through the word of God and actions amends all broken edges. The fact remains, you are not confident that the guy or girl next door will not cheat on you or hurt you. No one knows until one gets into the new marriage or home, thus the reason you should learn the necessary skills that will enable you to sustain your already existing home.

Secondly, the society frowns at an individual that marry others solely to get their residence permit in that country, which is the reason the immigration rules keep changing to make sure you have a good number of years with your spouse before you gain your residence permit.

Work as a team

Making your relationship open to family and friends, or official by getting married, enables both parties to work together as a team. At least you guys are responsible for each other based on an agreement made through a wedding, engagement or word of mouth.

Remedy: Working as a team is essential for a good marriage. There is a saying that two heads are better than one. Also, the Bible records in Amos 3:3, can two walk together, except they agree. Agreement between couples in anything makes that relationship a heaven on earth. Furthermore, any team that is united at work and decides pertaining any issues gains maximum result in business and profits, sometimes called like minds.

Grounded

The feeling of being grounded will help you know this is my man and this is my woman so keep off! You feel grounded or rooted when your family and friends become aware of the relationship by either engagement or marriage.

Remedy: Do not waste your time with someone you know you cannot marry. Kindly let go of any relationship that you are sure is leading nowhere because that will save you time and give you time to find another who will help you feel grounded by engagement or taking you to the altar.

Prove a point

Often, you hear people say that I want to show her that I can marry too, or I want to prove to my family that I am now a responsible man or woman! It is unwise to marry because you want to prove a point to your family or friends. Your achievements in life, whether marriage or career, speaks for you. You do not need to prove a point to anybody.

Remedy: Ignore pressure from family or friends. Focus on the real deal which is God and your search for that right spouse. Your life is unique, and you are not in competition with nobody. Always have that at the back of your mind.

Companionship

Having someone to chat with and share your issues with is a significant reason people marry or go into a relationship. Here, your husband or wife shares their experiences and stories daily with you. Most often than not, we confuse the word companion for sex. Being someone's companion is much more than sex, it involves spending quality time with the person which might include sex as well as eating, travelling and working hand in hand. Companionship kind of relationship is usually found amongst older couple because they may not be so sexually active, but they still spend quality time together.

Remedy: The remedy for this one is for us to be a real soul mates to our spouses. Spend time with your spouse always and make it a quality one still.

I will not judge anyone who decides to date, marry or go into a relationship because of the above reasons but my question is what if this attribute disappears in the future? For example, a guy that used to be rich becomes poor, or a woman that used to be beautiful gets old? What then happens to the relationship or union? Developing, nurturing and guiding your feelings for someone is important because change must occur and it's a conscious effort to keep loving and appreciating each other amid shifts in a relationship or marriage.

Types of marriage according to condition

The condition in this context refers to the state of that home. You will notice that this form comes from what is prevalent in that house. For example, enduring marriage means that couple is bearing and managing each other's excesses.

#Enduring marriage

Enduring marriage is common in homes that try to hold onto their marriage, not because they are happy or still in love, but because they have to keep the family name going, or maybe they want to protect their kids. Here, couples sometimes have their minds fixed on others outside. It could be the man is cheating, and vice versa. One evident fact is that the couple are not happy being with each other. Enduring marriage has two types.

One-sided

One-sided marriage is where the man or woman is holding the home. That is the wife or husband who is the one that tries to pursue peace or make peace all the time. I hear folk affirm to the fact that one person needs to keep the home. No! I believe that it is the duty of both the man and woman to maintain the home because the individual trying to ensure peace will get fed up one day which might lead to a drastic decision.

Two-sided

Here, both parties work to endure each other's excesses; they are also willing to stay for days without speaking to each other. They harbour unforgiveness in their hearts which can damage the home at any given opportunity.

#Ceremonial marriage

In this type of union, everything is official or formal between the couple. They neither have right or wrong times because there is no relationship at all. I called it ceremonial because they perform a duty in front of people, claiming that all is well. They go to church, occasionally just to fulfil all righteousness so that people would not notice what is going on with no strings attached. As soon as they come back home, everyone goes back to their rooms. This type of marriage is on the verge of breaking up.

#Modest marriage

A perfect home is the kind of union 'Relate With Me' encourages us to follow. It's a home where God is the decision maker, a home without blemish, a God's kind of home. Someone might ask is there such as a perfect home? My answer is yes! What you see is what you get, hence what do you visualise in your home? By faith and hard work, a modest marriage is possible. A modest marriage means relating to your spouse, and it involves a continuous improvement on relationships; by working on those little habits that want to destroy your union.

'Perfection' is about continuous improvement because when a couple in this category falls out, this couple always finds a way to make up before 24 hours elapses, and they follow the 'Forgiveness golden rule' which states that you should forgive each other seventy times seven, equals continuous forgiveness (Matthew 18:22). I know that forgiveness is not easy because human nature won't permit you to let go when you are hurt. However, with the help of God, it becomes easy.

The attributes of a modest home is:

- Prayer
- Commitment
- Forgiveness
- Honesty
- Transparency
- Mutual respect
- Mindful of words
- Communication

Praying

'Prayer' is an important tool for a good relationship. Committing one another's strengths and weaknesses in prayers will enable us to have a sustainable love for each other. Most married people see themselves as another man or woman in a dream; it's just a dream! A month later, their marriage crumbles because they did not pray against it. Let's learn to pray for one another. However, without choosing to work out love, prayer will be fruitless.

Commitment

The choice as to whether your relationship will work or not is in your hands. Engagement in relationships and marriage is a conscious effort. The question is, what am I doing wrong? Self-evaluate your character regularly to ascertain if you're working out your relationship or destroying it. If it ends up not working out, at least you will congratulate yourself knowing that you gave it your best shot. To date, I ask myself every day, "What haven't I done right?" because that will help shape my relationship, though it's not automatic, you have to start from somewhere. Another major important tip is 'Letting go'.

Forgiveness

There is no relationship or marriage without forgiveness. Most of us still recount what our Spouse did to us years ago, getting upset that very moment as if the incident just occurred. Don't get me wrong, sometimes we might need to discuss some of our past issues during a reasonable conversation, but a scenario where you get upset based on a matter of the past as though it were present is worrisome. That explains the fact that you haven't let go. I see most women waiting to pay their spouse or partner in their coin because there lies their peace of mind. To be honest, when you don't 'let go', you have no peace. I am saying this one from my experience, hence I made up my mind to either discuss the issue or consciously and prayerfully let go. Nothing on this earth is worth more than our peace of mind.

Trust

Trust only means having a level of belief in your partner. Trusting your partner is essential because no relationship can stand without it. The idea that your partner cannot hurt or cheat on you is a right approach instead of having to suspect every move he or she makes. To be honest, it's important to put your eyes to the ground while in a relationship or marriage. However, excessive nosing around your partner's phone and every move he or she makes can cause more harm than good.

Honesty

Someone that tells the truth is an honest person. Being truthful is another factor that can sustain and strengthen love. If your partner observes you tell lies, then to trust you becomes a difficult task. No wonder, the saying that 'trust is like a mirror, it can't get fixed because it's cracked'. Kindly tell the truth to always to avoid cracks in your relationship or marriage.

Transparency

When your partner sees the truth in you, then you're transparent. Please consult the difference between honesty and openness. Someone is seamless if the person is 'open'. Your partner should be able to have access to your phone when necessary to avoid any feeling of insecurity. Also, you should be able to take your calls freely before your partner, thus strengthening and sustaining the love between both of you.

Mutual respect

Respect means putting into consideration another person's feelings, wishes or rights. Respect becomes mutual when it's derived from two people. In this context, it will work with man and woman, the need for couples to have mutual respect for one another. Considering what your spouse feels or thinks is an important attribute or behaviour in a marriage or relationship. Sometimes, you find out that a man in a relationship wants to have his way all the time. He does not care about what the other thinks or not; all he worries about his selfish interest in any matter. Such men have no respect or regard for the feeling of their spouse, and that is not a useful attribute to have in a marriage. Couples should consider putting each other's desires first before achieving anything in life; it is called 'teamwork' and 'individual work.'

Mindful of your words

Your words are more powerful than anything. Spoken words will not be retrieved. What you say to your spouse can either make or mar your relationship. Kind and loving words such as "I love you," "Thank you," "You are beautiful," are recommended on a daily basis in relationships. You cannot afford to stop saying it. You need to keep topping up your love with sweet and romantic words. On the other hand, harsh words are a significant destroyer of a relationship. For example, in the past, I used to be careless with my words to my husband when I am angry. Once I am in a bad mood, I will always use words that I regret afterwards. It became a burden in my heart, and I started praying to God about that attribute. Through the word of God, prayers and holy spirit, I began to keep mute when my mood was not right. Silence, walking away nicely, speaking less, moving the discussion to a different time, became a thing of the day for me. And honestly, my marriage has not been the same since.

I felt I was free, I mean it's my husband, I have a right to tell him exactly how I feel. There is no need hiding my feeling towards him but no! That was a wrong approach. Yes, be free to communicate your feelings and thoughts to your spouse. However, be sensitive enough to know that your words might hurt him or her. I think we should roll our tongue ten times before you speak to your spouse especially in the heat of an argument or when you are angry. My advice is not to involve yourself in conversations that are leading nowhere. You will know undoubtedly when a discussion with your spouse is not making headway at the moment. Change the topic or be calm and let your spouse win just for peace to reign and to avoid using hurtful words.

Communication

Sometimes in marriages, couples tend to bottle up a lot on their mind against their partners because of the following:

- Fear of their spouse's reaction
- They do not want to cause problems
- They are making plans for revenge
- Their personality does not permit them to speak out for themselves
- They are in an abusive marriage, and much more.

Let me make it clear that there is no relationship without communication. Your spouse sometimes might not notice your actions or moods, and you need to speak out for yourself.

There are so many factors you need to consider before you bring up an issue before your partner:

- Consider the mood of your spouse
- Your choice of words
- The right location

Ask yourself questions such as:

- Should I wait until we get to bed?
- Is what I want to say necessary
- Is it something I can just let go of without thinking?
- How often has it occurred?
- Can I put the issues in prayers rather than talk?
- Have I complained about this before and what was the outcome?

Answering the above questions will enable you to know how to communicate rightly with your spouse. Good communication involves 'saying the right words, at the right time, with the right tone, with the right expression and in the right scenario'. Anything outside the above box is not considered fit for purpose regarding communication. Enduring, modest and ceremonial marriages have their similarities and differences. One significant similarity between the three categories of marriage is that they face challenges in different areas. The difference is that the problems are handled differently by the couple.

In summary:

Similarities
- Face challenges
- Fall out sometimes
- Agree sometimes

Differences
- Couples tackle issues differently
- Falling out lasts longer in enduring marriages than in modest marriages
- Forgiveness is easy in modest marriages than in enduring marriage marriages (forgiveness takes ages in enduring marriages)
- Couples in ceremonial marriages might be working towards divorce. There is no room for discussion, with everyone's mind made up.

What kind of marriage does 'Relate With Me' want?
- A home that accepts each other's personality without always pointing the finger
- A home that corrects through prayers, forgiveness and dialogue
- A marriage based on pure love that is God's kind of love
- A home that involves teamwork and commitment

Types of marriage according to time

Marriage is further divided or categorised by the time you get married. It could be early or late.

Early Marriage
Getting married early can be quite challenging for both the man and woman especially if both parties are not mature enough to handle the relationship. However, age is a number which means that managing a successful marriage at an early age depends on the mindset of the couple. Some people think that marrying at an early age might stop one from enjoying the kind of life he or she prefers. My question is what kind of enjoyment is that? Most women, especially those who married early, have this mentality that they did not enjoy their lives before getting married. In life, you cannot have it all. It doesn't matter the position you find yourself; if you married early or late, the bottom line is the fact that you decided to make your marriage work by putting in the effort. Some people are

of the opinion that more early marriages fail than late marriages. I disagree with that because any marriage can fail depending on the couple and their level of commitment to God (who should be the head of the home). Couples that have put in the effort to resolve their problems tend to save their homes. However, if the couple is not able to handle the issue, this could bring about divorce. From my view, it doesn't make sense dwelling on the time you married or not. Our focus is to make it work, no excuses or regrets, unless of course, the union has no remedy. Most problems in our homes are not early or late marriages or age. The primary issue is us. No need blaming 'Mr A' or 'Mrs A'! What are we doing to make it work? Stop pointing fingers and make it work unless both parties have unanimously agreed that the relationship cannot work, then no problem. If a couple still wants to be together, there is no need wasting each other's time by fighting every day. Deal with the issue prayerfully.

Advantages of early marriage:

- Escape heartbreaks
- Have children early
- Helps organise your life
- You learn in marriage

Disadvantages of early marriage:

- Sometimes feel left out which doesn't make sense. It is just a feeling
- Might not be mature enough to handle issues right
- Might have to multi-task

Late Marriage

Advantages of late marriage:

- Experience could make partners wise
- It's solely your decision
- You might have developed in career and otherwise

Disadvantages of late marriage:

- Having kids late which can be challenging
- Submission might be painful because you have made most of your decisions alone for a long time

Marriage according to location

Distance marriage is when a couple does not live together due to one reason or the other. It could be because of the nature of the wife's or husband's job or any other reason. It's hard for a long-distance marriage to survive but it has its pros or cons. However, the disadvantages of a couple living apart are high. Relationships always work better when people see each other. That's not to say that being apart is entirely wrong; sometimes it helps strengthen the love between couple thereby making them miss each other, hence valuing each other more.

Eight ways to survive in the long-distance marriage

Communication

The couple must have excellent communication systems such as Skype, telephone, WhatsApp, Facebook. Thank goodness the world has gone global; social media is there to help couples see and communicate to another without feeling much of the person's absence. Couples should use social media daily unless otherwise stated. The use of Skype and telephones can help couples bond together more, and both parties look forward to meeting each other daily. Someone might ask what if there is no network coverage in the area? There is always a way around everything. You must consciously find a location that has network coverage at least once a week where you can send emails, messages or even a voice message. Be aware that lack of communication can ruin the relationship as you do not know what your partner is doing and the mind can be deceptive. Constant communication will help you know that your partner has not ditched you for another, enhancing the sense of security.

Right words

It's one thing to communicate, and it's another thing to say the right words. 'Right words' in this context mean always approaching your spouse with words that can keep the person going such as "I love you," "I miss you," "Don't worry, the distance is not forever."

For women, do not nag your husband over the phone as he might misinterpret it. From my experience, the way my spouse reacts to comments I make is different from when I text it or speak to him over the phone. He always laughs and views some statements I make as jokes. However, if I make the same comment on the phone or text it to him, he gets upset and thinks that I am being rude. Try complaining about something over the phone and check your spouse's reaction. Also, do it face to face; you will understand what I mean.

Set out time/time management

It's important to set aside a time of the day where you can connect with your spouse either through phone, laptop or any other social media. Time management is crucial, especially if you guys are going to be apart for a while. Please be advised to keep to these hours unless something urgent comes up. Do not try to do other things during that period unless permitted by the other party. For instance, if you are on Skype with your spouse and chatting on the phone with another person. Now that can be annoying because that is supposed be your set aside time or what I call BONDING

TIME, where you get to catch up on the day's events and do your daily gossips. Focusing on your partner for that period will help prevent arguments and unnecessary fights.

Avoid prolonged silence/argument

Sometimes, couples fall out. Some quarrels strengthen love and togetherness. However, kindly avoid cases when you are apart because you cannot see the person to know how this person feels. Some folk hurt each other in an angry or emotional state. Maybe your spouse might try to seek solace in some friend or colleague somewhere because of your prolonged silence or lack happiness each time you guys talk. Also, beware that the devil always comes into a relationship especially marriage when there is anger, hatred, sorrow and bitterness. Do not take this negative attribute to bed. He doesn't dwell in a place where righteousness, peace, and joy because that's the Kingdom of God. Let's not be ignorant of his tactics because Bible posits that:

'He is moving around looking for whom to devour.'
1 Peter 5:8

I will rephrase that part of the scripture as 'He is moving around looking for where to plant bitterness.'

I have heard so many stories of how some women slept with another man during her lowest state of mood, hence cheating on their partner and causing more harm than good to the relationship. Pursue peace with your partner daily, apologise when you need to, even if it's a text message. The magic words such as "sorry," "thank you," "please" will help in amending whatever the disagreement or quarrel. Don't use these words when it's too late, use them as early as possible.

Prayer

What you cannot do physically for your spouse, prayer will cover. For instance, you cannot stop your wife or husband from cheating on you but prayer can. Honestly, it's hard to tell what he or she is doing. Your partner can still cheat on you. If you decide to 'set out time', 'communicate,' use 'the right word' and praying 'deaf ears to side talks'. You have to consistently ask God to secure your man or woman to help him or her never to succumb to any testing that will be to the detriment of your union. Prayer is key to everything, trust me on that.

Listening to side talks

We sometimes are not aware that many are not happy about their relationship with their wife or husband. It's not only the devil that is running looking for homes to attack but human beings too. This kind of people can be your best friend, relatives, work colleague, parents, or even your siblings. Some of them are out to ruin your home, and you may be unaware. That doesn't mean that they cannot be right at times but investigate and carefully find out from your spouse if what anybody says about him or her is accurate before concluding. That way, you do not have issues or lose your partner's trust due to insecurity. Be willing to forgive if your suspicion is right as the girl or guy next door might not be better off after all – having a robust and weak point which explains the fact that no one is perfect, including you.

Plan visiting

Always plan to visit each other as that will help sort a lot which social media and prayer cannot do. Marriage encourages a couple to live together - two shall become one, both spiritually and physically. Endeavour to save up money and book holidays at work just to see your spouse. Please don't leave it for too long; there must be a way around this things. Visiting could go along to settle disputes and increase bonding, which will keep you both going to the next meeting. The ways for survival have to go hand in hand. No one can survive without the other. If you always pray for your spouse without trying to visit once in a while, you might lose out and vice versa.

Be happy

Always make yourself comfortable when you're apart. Do not revolve your life around the fact that your partner is not there because you will end up being sad which will affect your relationship. There must be a particular reason why you guys are apart; focus on the benefit as well as do the things you enjoy most. For example, hang out with genuine friends and family, go to watch movies or go to church, listen to music you enjoy. What are your hobbies? Make your day fun to avoid drilling him or her over the phone or on Skype. Engaging yourself helps you have stories to tell your partner during the meeting time.

Benefits of long-distance marriage:

- You can achieve a lot when your partner is not around. I get so distracted from writing if my partner is with me and vice versa.
- It will help you appreciate whatever your spouse used to do for you, especially the house chores and school runs which you now have to do alone.
- It helps the couple to discuss better with each other, giving every needed detail. You might have a less broad conversation when you're together.
- It tests your level of trust and patience. If your marriage can survive distance, be assured that it can withstand any issues.
- Distance will teach you how to handle urgent issues without any support from your spouse.
- It enables couples to value the time spent together as you're not sure of the next meeting.
- Opportunity to travel often and a change of environment:

You might not plan trips or holiday on an average day, but with the distance, couples might be forced to move often just to be together, hence exposing you to different locations and scenarios depending on where your spouse lives.
- It can be fun planning on how to spend time with your partner. I remember when my husband was away for six weeks. I prepared for his return.

21 major causes of problems in marriages for both early and late marriage and its remedies

There are many causes of problems in homes and marriages, but I will divide them into major and minor issues. The major issues are those issues that have destroyed homes. That is not to say that the small problems do not damage homes. However, there is a higher tendency that the majors destroy relationships more than the minors. Both the major and minor problems affect marriages negatively, depending on the couple. Therefore, none of these issues should be underrated because it can destroy long-built unions.

Lack of forgiveness

What does forgiveness mean to you? Can I ever forgive my partner for hurting me?

Hmmmm! "I have forgiven you" It's easier said than done but it is achievable if you are willing and have the right tool.

Forgiveness for me is one of the most sensitive attributes I had to learn as a wife and mother. The ability to let go of past experiences is the number one attribute of a Christian.

Jesus said that 'God should forgive us even as we forgive those who trespass against us.' (Matthew 6:12) Therefore, if we do not forgive our partner, we cannot be overlooked by God.

One major issue we have in our homes today is the lack of forgiveness. The 'revenge syndrome' is the order of the day in most of our relationships. I have met folk in life that can never have peace until they have retaliated what you did to them even if it takes them years to achieve. Please be advised that forgiveness is a process; it's not automatic especially if the hurt is deep. For instance, if you start working out in the gym today, you do not expect six packs to appear on your body overnight. Time and making effort are reliable weapons in achieving forgiveness.

Here are some tips which have helped me realise remission in the past years:

- Pray for grace to forgive as you cannot do it on your own.
- Forgive yourself. I have scenarios where I kept feeling sorry for what I did or did not do. We should learn first to forgive ourselves for areas we are not holding right.
- Identify your grudge and deal with it as early as possible as procrastination prolongs issues.
- Accepting your partner's personality and be aware that everyone is different, thus, react to problems differently.
- Practice showing love and mercy (Blessed are the merciful for they shall obtain mercy, Matthew 5:7).
- Eradicate pride and superiority (humility is a significant sign of forgiveness).
- Start the discussion in a peaceful mood having the intention of reconciliation, not a fighting attitude.
- Do not mix up the conversation with other past issues. Instead, take each topic one after the other.
- Give room for turn talking because that will help for clarity.
- Proper analysis of what is happening in your partner's life will enable you to let go of any grudge. For example, your partner's stressful job can affect his or her behaviour towards you. Show empathy towards your spouse because that will enable you to overlook any hurt and to forgive.

Forgiveness has significant advantages which can help build a lasting relationship. Some of these advantages are below:

- Creates peaceful atmosphere which is right (especially individuals with kids)
- Enhances unity which increases blessings
- Your heart becomes free (improve good health)
- Sleep better because you're no longer angry or worried about whatever that happened
- Happiness
- Gives you self-esteem and strength to push ahead in life
- It helps prevent unhealthy anger, sadness (depression) and worry

The main disadvantage of not forgiving is the lack of peace of mind which affects your ability to concentrate on other issues of life. You can apply the above tips to your relationship with relatives and friends, not just your partner. So guys, pray about whatever your partner did to you and ask God for grace on how to express yourself to avoid any issues and trust me, you will be amazed at the outcome.

Hanging around your ex

Most of us have another best friend apart from our spouse. We need to make our spouses our best friend. Don't get me wrong, we can have good friends who we can discuss issues with, but our spouses should be our best friends. Your ex is called ex (a person you used to love), past 'used to' and not present.

Infidelity

Cheating on each other is an important trigger to marital issues. When you start sleeping with someone that is not your spouse, you might begin to compare them to your spouse as well as complaining about things that you never really noticed in your spouse.

Bad habits

A bad habit is an undesirable conduct pattern. For example, shouting while speaking can be a habit which one partner may not fancy. Other examples include overspending, procrastination and much more.

Money

As the saying goes, money is the root of all evil. Finance is one of the most common causes of problems in homes. No woman will like to suffer or not to have her primary need met. However, marriage is for better for worse. We should learn to support one another whether there is money or not. Money is not everything, but it can help keep you comfortable.

Health

Many people have left their spouses because of health issues. Imagine if you were the one in that person's shoes? How will you feel? Some men go around to sleep with other women because their spouse has just had a baby. That is annoying because the baby she had is for both of you and if her body changes, it wasn't her making.

Praying

A family that stays together, prays together. Lack of prayer in a home can destroy the home because a prayerful home is robust and can withstand any obstacles in life.

Logic

Logic comes in when either both couples are logically thinking. Such people with a logical mindset say, "This is how it should be, so therefore, I cannot do this." You wronged me so you should be the one apologising. Sometimes this pattern of life destroys a home because no one is willing to accept responsibility.

Lazy

Some of us are lazy; we don't want to work or even help with house chores. Some women stay at home and spend without earning. Also, some men refuse to help with tasks claiming a woman has to take care of the home.

No love

When there is no love in the air in any home, then the marriage is as good as dead. Couples that love each other do have issues, let alone the ones that does not love each other. When you love someone, tolerating the person's excesses becomes easy, but when you don't like your spouse, everything the person does becomes a problem.

Lack of sex

When a spouse is not satisfied in bed with your sexual performance, it becomes an issue. We need to communicate with each other and let our spouse know how we feel about our sex lives. Let him or her know that you are not enjoying the pattern. Have an agreement on what style best suits both parties.

Common problems in bed:

- Lack of satisfaction
- Reduced libido after childbirth (see my story of having a baby)
- Premature ejaculation
- Different sexual position
- Having a routine with sex/missionary journey

Lack of children

When a couple spends so many years trying for a child, that can cause a significant problem in the relationship, thus making either of the couple to seek for a solution outside their homes or from the wrong sources.

Selfishness

Most times we think a lot of ourselves. Remember love is not selfish. You have to consider your spouse in whatever you do. I am not saying that you should kill yourself for anybody. However, some people think about only themselves without understanding the feelings of their spouse before doing something.

Relatives/third party

Do not put your family and friends before your spouse. Never allow your mum, sister, brother or father to run your home for you. That is the reason they are called extended family members. Bring them into your issues when you both have agreed on who to contact or in extreme cases but not for problems you are aware that both can handle. You can seek help if the problem gets out of hand.

Stress

Workloads, schools and taking care of the children can bring pressure in couples. We should co-operate with one another during this trying time. Having an understanding that your spouse is stressed can help. However, the stressed partner should be aware that the other has a need. Be careful to separate stress and to give attention to your spouse.

Competition

Competing with your spouse has been a significant issue in most homes. Do not be offended if your spouse earns more than you. The money he or she is making is for the good of the family. So be happy for him or her, don't feel that my wife earns more than I do so let me cut off her wings and make her know that I am better. Some couple tends to compete with themselves. The Bible says that two shall become one (Mark 10:8). Whatever your spouse has is for you. Please be advised that you are not competing with yourselves. Support one another in all endeavours and play your role accordingly.

Lack of trust

Suspicion can kill a home. When you don't trust your spouse, the centre cannot hold. Every male folk around your wife is a suspect or wants to sleep with your wife and vice versa.

Appearance

Take care of your body and look good always. Don't go bed at night without having a shower. Make sure to dress well at all times. Some men have been put off by their wife's appearance, so be careful how you wear, especially women.

Bad friends

The Bible (1 Corinthians 15:33) records that evil communication corrupts right manner. You need to be careful of the kind of friends you have or associate with because that can go a long way to affect your relationship with your spouse. If you have friends that always talk about divorce, there is a high tendency that you will do the same as well. Choose your friends and don't let them choose you.

Lack of communication

Where there is no communication, there is no marriage. Lack of communication is a significant factor that can destroy a home.
Misunderstanding in relationships is as a result of lack of discussions between couples.

Pride

Pride is a primary cause of so many issues in life, not just marriage but in any relationships. No wonder the Bible says that God resists the proud and gives grace to the humble (James 4:6). Some people find it difficult to use the magic word "I love you, "I am sorry," and "Thank you."

Lack of patience

Impatience has killed so many homes today, and it is a significant challenge because we need the patience to overcome the issues that come up in our relationships. We need to learn patience with our spouses. I know sometimes it is not easy but it's worth it. For example, tolerance covers up what we can no longer bear.

Third party

Most times, we tend to run to our parents or friends each time we have an issue with our spouse. I know in some extreme cases we might need help. Let's quit the habit of running around to a third party at the slightest opportunity.

Anger

I remember, as humans, we get angry sometimes but don't let it last for long. I used to struggle with anger a lot, but God has been helping me, and by God's grace, it is working. Significant to control your anger is by acknowledging that it is your weakness, praying, keeping mute or maybe walking away.

Lack of self-confidence

When you feel the need to be admired by someone that is not your partner which could mean your partner does not tell you how beautiful you are. Some women love to be admired and appreciated; they feel less loved if their husband does not respect them, which in turns destroys their union.

Lack of support

Everyone wants someone that will help fulfil his or her destiny. No one wants to be married to someone that does not encourage one's career, business, skills, house chores and other areas of life as the case may be. Not giving maximum support to your spouse sometimes is a major destroyer of your relationship. Imagine a scenario where you are handling a project, and all you get is negative comments from your spouse with no form of support. Bear in mind that supporting your spouse to achieve his or her dream comes in diverse ways. You can render support to your spouse through...

Indirect support

- Words of advice
- Helping to buy materials needed for the person's project or career
- Starting up a business
- Paying fees

Direct support

Direct support is when you get involved in any project being handled by a spouse. For example, if your husband makes clothes or is a fashion designer, you can help him or her by cutting some materials, putting needles together, ironing the clothes for clients or, better still, help take care of the kids while he makes the clothes. Another direct support you can give to your spouse is praying for the person always to prosper.

Support is classified into...

Career support

Helping your spouse in his or her career is actualised by finding out what you can do to make their workload easier. For example, you could help your spouse gather sources of data for research. Collecting the data will enable your husband or wife to focus on the investigation, thus making life easier for them.

House chore support

House chore support comes into play when you do not have a nanny or a helper to do house works such as cleaning, cooking, washing up, cleaning the bathroom and kitchen, and so on. I know that women take care of that part of the family more than men. However, every woman will appreciate a husband that gives her a hand in making the house organised for everyone. Giving your spouse a helping hand to run the family makes life easy for everyone and that will decrease the level of stress

No love

Often, we confuse the word 'love' for 'romance', although I am certain they go together but they are not the same. Loving your partner can be seen in a different dimension. Some people think that 'love' is 'affection' whereas others believe that love is 'romance' or perhaps 'sexual desire'. One unique thing about this perception is that no one can feel it with bare hands. Therefore, love starts with the mind or as a thought which has the strength and influences your behaviour towards another. This act comes into play when you respect, care, support, forgive and adore your partner.

I hear folks say that love is blind. From my perspective, love not only has eyes but ears and nose. That's why you notice and get upset when your partner or spouse hurts you. A 'blind love' does not see wrong or hurt, thus it accepts a partner's personality or everything he or she does without grudge. Love is essential in every relationship, it may not be enough on its own to sustain a relationship but is one of the reasons to stay in your marriage. "I love my wife or husband," - I am sure you have heard that a couple of times from folks. In a situation where the feeling of love is no more in your home, it becomes an issue, and everyone starts to struggle. Let us look at love from a diverse perspective.

Understanding love from a biblical perspective

Sometimes we claim we love someone without understanding the real meaning of love. I'm not writing about theology, but I cannot correctly discuss love without referring to the book of all books, the Bible, which posits that;

'Love is enduring, love is kind. It does not envy; it does not brag, it is not proud. It is not impolite, it is not self-seeking, it is not easily angered, and it keeps no account of wrongs.'
1 Corinthians 13:4-5

If I claim to love my spouse, I should be able to exhibit all of the above qualities or work hard towards achieving them. I just thought it would be helpful to encourage us today to have a proper think about what love means to us using the Bible as a template. And, while you may love your partner, do you like yourself?

Keeping the fire burning in marriage

Marriage is a long-term affair and needs efforts on the part of the man and the woman to keep the fire of love burning and avoid dull moments. Some women have this ideology that their husbands are not attracted to them after marriage. Below are tips that help a woman stayed attracted to the husband after the wedding.

Reasons a man will be attracted to his wife after marriage

I would say that some people are attracted to their wives after the wedding, but some men are not. It depends on what the man wants in a woman and if the woman is keeping up to speed in every area of her life and career. The question for me is what will keep a man less or more attracted to his wife after marriage?
    A man could be:

Sexually attracted

When a man gets turned on by the wife, and he always desires to make out with the woman, then it's obvious he is attracted sexually to the woman. In this case, the woman needs to keep their bedroom light burning by always charging the battery of their sexual life.

Physically attracted

This kind of attraction has to do with your physique. Your looks are essential in a marriage or relationship. Some men might be attracted to their wife based on the physical appearance.

Financially attracted

Some men may not be attracted to their wives because they are of no economic importance to them whereas other people will love their wives irrespective of their financial status. Some women gain the loyalty of their spouse because of her financial position in the home.

Spiritually attracted

Some men are happy when they find out that their wife loves God, obey his commandment as well as work in the church for God. If a husband loves God, he will be happy if you love God as well.

Intelligence attraction

Some men are attracted to women that are very intelligent. No man wants a dummy for a wife. However, it's unfortunate that some guys feel intimidated if their woman happens to be smarter than them. These set of people are only jealous. Instead, they should enjoy and be proud of whom their wives have become.

Behaviour attraction

Your man could be attracted to you because you have good manners and you respect him, and others put into consideration your children's and family's well-being. However, the man could be less attracted to you if you don't show love or care for him, your children and others. This behaviour has to do with your character in and outside your home. Find below a summary of what can keep a man attracted to you.

24 ways you can keep your man attracted to you:

- Physical attraction
- Spiritual affinity
- Behavioural attraction
- Look good
- Behave well
- Pray for your spouse to remain attracted to you
- Be romantic
- Show him love but don't be stupid
- Respect him in his way. This is difficult sometimes because men see respect differently from women
- Love his family and friends

- Apply wisdom when advising him about his family and friends
- Cover up for him: they hate their flaws to be exposed
- Do your chores yourself because they might use it against you, even when they claim not to
- Be open to your spouse but careful what you tell him about your friends. He might start thinking the same applies to him
- Do not discuss your spouse with friends, but trusted family members
- Don't have secrets but don't vomit yourself to him, some women's stories are just not necessary information for him
- Make him feel in charge even though you earn more
- Don't challenge him
- Do not be too comfortable that you know your spouse; don't be negative but expect changes
- Care for your children
- Don't be a talkative but be humorous
- Work on your sex life; create new sex tricks
- Keep yourself happy always because this will help your spouse and family remain delighted
- Keep up your level of intelligence

I will encourage a continuous improvement on relationships which includes keeping to the above rules as much as you can. The above guidelines will enable your man remains attracted to you. The dynamics between women and men have recently changed drastically, as the women have proved that they are capable of doing almost everything that men can do and that too in a far better manner. In fact, modern women are balancing their home and work as well as doing every task which comes their way. However, the actual equality between women and men will take place only when both of them say and do the same things for one another, hence with the help of this book, you will come to understand a few loving stuff, which every man should often say to his woman.

I cannot take my eyes off you!

After a hard day at work, both at home as well as in the office, every woman wants to hear something romantic from her partner and what else than telling them how beautiful they look.

We will eat together when the food is ready!

Gone are the days when a wife has to starve until the husband had the lunch/dinner. With the changing times, a man should try and eat together with his woman whenever the meal is ready.

I am right here if you need me!

Irrespective of the level of work a woman does in her office or to meet requirements of the family, she needs support from the person whom she loves the most, hence a man should often say and express his moral support by saying that he is right there whenever she needs him.

I saw this dress and bought it for you. You'll look lovely in it!

Even though a woman has plenty of formal, casual, trendy and stylish dresses worth a million dollars in her wardrobe, the dress gifted by her life partner is valuable for her. A man should buy a cute dress (based on his own choice) for his woman and praise her for the beautiful look. Even if she does not like the dress, you can give her the option of choosing another dress that suits her taste.

Thanks for the dinner, it was delicious!

A man should always remember that his wife still prepares the food of his own choice despite the fact that she had tons of other work in her workplace or home. In this case, sometimes praising her meals by saying it was a delicious dinner or any other kind words will bring a smile to her face.

You are important to me!

Most women, irrespective of their profession, family background or anything else, desire to get attention from her spouse. Saying this quote for some time will give her a good value and retain a healthy relationship.

I will make tea today!

You can sometimes cook for your woman. Although women are known to prepare tea and other beverages at home, such gestures give relaxation to the women significantly. Also, when a man makes the meal, it reduces the stress off her and in return she will create more time to give her man maximum attention.

Do you want to dance with me?

There is nothing more special for a woman than the opportunity to dance with her life partner in a ballroom with music in the background, thus being a husband, you should schedule at least one day in a month to enjoy dancing with your partner. Call it a one-off treat!

Do whatever you want, it's your own life!

Real men/husbands always give respect to the feeling of their women and hence they do not put any restrictions in their lives. A man should always encourage his woman to do whatever makes her happy in life, as long as it does not hurt her life and society.

You are doing great at work. I am proud of you!

Other than household work, today, most of the women work in offices or as freelancers. While you praise her for a well-prepared meal, you should also appreciate your woman regarding her excellent job. Tell her you are proud of her achievement at work or in her career. Some women lose their self-confidence and feel less attractive, especially after having babies.

SECTION THREE
BABIES

Some women lose their self-confidence and feel less attractive after having babies. Babies are blessings from God which every woman appreciates but it comes with a lot of changes, both physically, emotionally and psychologically for the couple, especially the woman. As a result of marriage and sexual intimacy between couples, babies are the by-product. The coming of babies in a relationship brings changes to the relationship and, if not managed effectively, might cause more harm than good.

Strategies on how to deliver your baby alone

The inspiration to write this section came from my personal story. It was just two days until my due date, and my baby decided to come. My due date was on 2nd September 2016 and my baby came on 31st August. Having a baby in front of my staircase is one incident I cannot forget.

>There are three reasons I chose to use my story as an illustration:

- To encourage anyone who does not believe in God to be aware that he exists and protects.
- To advise pregnant women to always follow their instinct and never to leave the hospital if they do not feel comfortable.
- To give pregnant women tips on how to take care of their new arrival in case they come quickly.

On the night of 30th August around 11 pm, yours truly started having contractions without any show. I didn't wake my husband up because I was not sure if it was Braxton Hicks contractions or actual labour. The contractions increased and became fast, so I decided to call my mum who lives abroad. She monitored me and noticed that the contractions were coming every three minutes so she said we should start going to the hospital as my baby would arrive soon. I felt the same way too because I was already feeling the pressure to poo. Around 2 am I quickly woke my hubby up, changed, and dressed my two kids (7-year-old girl and three-year-old boy). We got to the hospital; the first midwife observed and asked me not to go to the toilet if I felt the pressure 'down below' as that could be the baby coming. She then handed me over to another midwife who came in again to observe me. She examined me. Her exact words were, "Your cervix is soft but your contractions, which are coming every three minutes, are not high enough, hence you're 1 cm dilated. The contractions might stop or increase so we can't keep you in the hospital." My spouse and I pleaded with her that I could not go back home because I live miles away but she insisted that we had to go. I spent a few minutes at the reception, then around 4 am, we decided to leave the hospital, which was a bad mistake.

When I got home, the pains became so strong, but I held onto the information that I was 1cm dilated. The urge to push became so intense that I told my partner to call the hospital to inform them that I could not manage the pain anymore. As he was about to go upstairs to get his phone, with a cloth tied round my waist, suddenly we heard a high sound! My waters broke. I was terrified, and we were confused. I encouraged him to call emergency. As he went upstairs, within few seconds my baby popped out on the floor in front of my staircase and the umbilical cord cut because I was standing when the baby dropped. I picked the baby up and sat on my staircase. My husband and kids came out staring at me in the pool of my blood and water. The emergency unit was called; they came 30 to 45 minutes after I had the baby. The good news is that nothing happened to me and the baby by the mercy of God, although he was kept in the incubator for 24 hours because he got a cold, but all thanks to God.

Ways to cope if you find yourself in such situation.

Call the hospital
This tip will be relevant if the baby decides to wait but my baby came before my partner went up to get his phone, as my waters broke immediately. However, call the emergency services for help in case your child isn't ready to come. Always make sure you have the right contact available.

Good position

When you feel the intense pressure to push, be advised that could be your baby coming so find the most comfortable position to avoid your child falling. Make sure the distance between your child and the bed or floor is at the minimum, although you might be in shock to know what's going on. But just remember my experience and search for the best position.

Strong urge to push

Do not hold back the urge to push as you might hurt your baby. Try your best to get yourself into a comfortable position and carefully push.

Umbilical cord

Avoid cutting the umbilical cord to prevent infection until you get medical support. And keep praying while you wait for help.

Move away

Carefully step away from the exact spot where you gave birth as there will be lots of germs as a result of broken water and blood from your body. Again, this will help avoid infection.

Protect the baby

Wrap the baby up immediately so as to avoid getting a cold. You can cover the child with a towel, bedsheet or any material you find safe enough at that moment pending when the ambulance arrives as they may not be quick.

Skin to skin

Hold your baby close to your skin to keep baby warm as you may not have anything to wrap the baby immediately when he or she is out. Remember the baby is placed on your body once he or she comes out by the midwife at the hospital so be conscious enough to do that.

Breastfeeding

Breastfeeding the baby will help him/her to relax before you get help from emergency unit. Avoid anything going into the mouth of the child apart from your nipple, and this will help prevent infection.

> **To avoid putting yourself and baby at risk:**
> - Plan for some helper four weeks before the due date especially if you have kids. You need to contact three to four friends and family to be on the safe side and to avoid any disappointment.
> - Follow your instinct when you're in labour.
> - Never leave the hospital no matter what any midwife says, unless contractions have stopped.
> - Make sure you are praying and stay positive.
>
> **How to avoid being traumatised:**
>
> Having an unplanned home birth can be quite traumatising. Here are ways that will help you overcome that challenge:

- Spend time with family and friends.
- Go out if you feel like it.
- Try to get help with the baby.
- Rest as often as possible.
- Pray always and stay active: that was my key to happiness and strength.
- Start doing the things you enjoy, such as playing music, dancing, reading, and singing. The above activities can help overcome depression and any psychological trauma.
- Eat well to avoid being weak especially during the period of breastfeeding.

Guidelines on how to take care of your baby during shopping

Children are a precious gift from God; how we care for the children, especially babies, matters a lot because of their vulnerability. Children do not grow on trees; they come as a result of an intimate sexual relationship between opposite genders. The principal caregiver is the mother, but there are babies whose mother has died during labour or when they were still tender, hence the reason they grew up with a foster mum or parents. In one scenario, a woman locked her few month old baby in a car and went into the shop to buy something, leaving her child in the care of no one. On getting to the store, she got carried away with the shopping and speaking to people. When she got back to her car, the baby was brought out by someone after the person broke into her car. So many people tried to help the baby while crying but they couldn't get the baby out because the car was locked, hence the reason they broke her door and called the police on her because the baby had died. Therefore, leaving your child in the car without any care is not an option. The first thing that came to my mind when I heard the scenario (a video) was "What would the baby's father say or think?" That can cause an issue in their marriage or relationship because that was a case of total negligence and the man might not be able to bear the pain or loss of their new baby.

Reasons you should not leave your baby in the car:
- To avoid suffocation
- Someone might take your child
- People can damage your car
- The police and social service might get involved
- Your child might get hungry
- Your baby might choke to death
- There might be a queue at the shop
- There might be a fire outbreak from the car
- It can cause a problem for you and spouse should something happens to the baby.

The risk involved in leaving your child in the car outweighs the convenience of going into the shops alone. Taking care of your child while shopping can be enough especially if your partner or spouse is not with you. There are many ways you can take care of your baby while you shop.

How to take better care of your baby outside without feeling the stress:

- Do not take the baby out and about if he or she has just been immunised or is not feeling too well.
- Make sure all the changing materials are with you especially items such as (nappies, wipes, sudocrem) etc.
- The baby should be well fed before leaving the house.
- Try to see if your child has a dirty nappy before leaving the house because this helps the baby feels relaxed when you are out and about.
- Take enough food and finger meals, depending on the age of the child.
- Go with strap, buggy and car seat to see which one is the most comfortable for you and the child at the shop.
- Give the baby their favourite toy to hold if he or she is teething. Also, that will keep them busy.
- Make sure you check the baby as often as possible especially his or her bum area so as to ascertain if the

baby needs a change of nappy or not.
- You can ask a friend or family to take care of the baby for a particular number of hours that will be suitable for the person. Be advised not to take too much time as the individual may not want to help you next time, unless you have a tangible reason such as traffic, queue, etc.
- If you are not a single parent, go shopping only when your spouse or partner is home to avoid taking the baby outside. You can follow this method if you have a massive amount of shopping to do or, better still, go with your wife or husband.
- You can also shop online which is easier depending on your location and where you shop. This can be delivered right to your doorstep.
- You can also shop more than once weekly and pick your items in small quantity so that you don't waste too much time at the shop which might make the baby get stressed out.
- Put your meal together in case you get hungry. Taking care of a child is sometimes demanding, so you need to make yourself as comfortable as possible before leaving the house for shopping. Babies disturb less if they get the adequate care needed unless there is something wrong health wise which you are not aware of, although this might not be the case. It is paramount you settle your baby before going out and about with them. I know that it is easier said than done because mothers get so busy with work, but it is worth the try.

Children

Getting married early can be quite challenging for both the men and women. However, age is just a number which means handling a successful marriage or relationship at a young age depends on the mindset of the couple. Some people think that marrying at a young age might stop one from enjoying the kind of life he or she prefers. Most women, especially those that married early, have this mentality that they did not enjoy your lives before getting married. Women that took their time before tying the knot sometimes have a lot to regrets and may have made some mistakes, whereas others are of the opinion that most early marriages fail than late marriage. I disagree with that because any marriage can fail depending on the couple and their level of commitment. It doesn't matter the position you find yourself, or if you married early or late; the bottom line is the fact that you decided to make your relationship work, especially with your partner and children. Couples or partners that have put in a lot of effort to resolve their problems tend to save their homes which create a better life and good living for the children, hence sustaining a healthy society and producing good leaders for a better tomorrow. It doesn't matter if the child has special needs or not; any child can be useful and a leader. The leadership starts from a good relationship, whether in marriage or relationship, as long as the child has a connection with the father and mother, receiving necessary care, support and love.

Children: A product of marriage and relationship

Most people get worried if they do not marry on time because they do not want to have children late. However, marrying at an early age is not a guarantee to have children early. Some women are mothers who did not marry but have children. It could be a personal decision or a mistake. Also, some women lost their husband early in the marriage. They were still able to take care of themselves and their children, maintaining a healthy relationship with people. If partners are not able to handle their differences, this could bring about divorce or separation. Separation has an adverse effect not only on the couple but the children. In fact, children of a separated couple bear the consequences more than the parents.

Effects of unhealthy relationship on children:

- Poor academic performance
- Depression which leads to an unhappy lifestyle
- Prefer their own company
- Meet the wrong friends
- Development might be affected
- Live a different life from the initial plan
- Affects them psychologically by keeping them in a distressed state.
- Poor relationship with friends, peers and family
- Could change the child's original personality

The above effects of unhealthy relationships on children are not always the case. However, it occurs in a majority of them. Children need their parents, especially their mother, for their personal development. According to John Bowlby in his 'attachment theory,' a child needs to have one main caregiver for his or her personal growth. 'Attachment theory' can be defined as a deep and emotional bond that connects two parties within a period and space (Bowlby 1969; Ainsworth 1973). John Bowlby, who has worked with emotionally distressed children as a psychiatrist in a child guidance Clinic in London, developed the 'attachment method'. John Bowlby, alongside James Robertson, observed the distressed state which was as a result of separation from their mothers, which brought about the importance of a mum in a child's life and development. However, Dollard and Miller (1950) are of the opinion in their 'behaviour theory of attachment' that a child does not require any bond or relationship with their mother for efficient development, thus a child needs the care of both father and mother for their personal growth, because in life every caregiver has a role to play directly or indirectly on the personal development of the child (Ricther, L. 2004).

An adult or a parent can be said to have exhibited a level of attachment to the child when he or she responds to the needs of a child appropriately, by being sensitive enough to identify this need (Bowlby 1969). For instance, based on my experience as a child, I grew up with a single mother, and I will agree that a child requires not only the mother for personal development but the father. Although my mother was able to take care of us like any parent would, I watched her struggle. A little of my history... I am a product of a single parent but am useful today by God's grace. My dad died when I was just two weeks old, leaving my mum with three kids (girls). She became a widow after five years of marriage. She was able to achieve that by God's grace, she says. My mum was able to reach that by identifying two needs - the children and her needs appropriately, and although this was not an easy process, God was on her side.

Identified needs for children and herself:

- Standard education
- Provision of meals
- Emotional support
- Spiritual support (Christian beliefs and taking us to church)
- Building a rapport with her kids at tender age
- Offering relevant advice as and when required
- Joining forum of like minds such as church groups
- Participated in singing which was her hobby
- Denied herself of an expensive lifestyle and luxury

Whether you are a single mum or married, the bottom line is to have a healthy relationship with:

- the family especially children because a healthy relationship affects the lives and behaviour of children;
- peers;
- friends;
- business associate; and,
- colleagues.

The above tips can help any single mum or widow to take care of their children. The society will be a better place if our kids live a better life and have a sense of inclusion, especially children with special needs. While growing, children copy behaviour from parents, especially as babies, before they get into peer group mirroring and society (Berk 2012).

That is the reason we as parents should be careful how we handle our:

- daily activities;
- behaviour;
- relationships with spouses; and,
- contact with our children.

For example, a mother tends to have a high tone of voice when she speaks to her seven-year-old. One day, the seven-year-old was caught talking the same way to her younger brother, a three-year-old, saying, "Stop it!" The caregiver could hear herself speaking through the little girl. The girl interprets her caregiver's behaviour, and she is now careful how she treats her kids. She learnt how to manage her tone while speaking because this will help the little girl in the future. Most adults' behaviour in their marriage or relationship is as a result of what they saw their parents/guardians exhibit during their childhood. If their parents verbally abused each other while they grew up, they begin to see that as a way of life. You automatically take that with you as an adult into your marriage or relationship.

Children with special needs

Children with disabilities will be able to have a real life and not feel excluded from the society if they grow up in the right environment, with the right relationship with their parents or caregivers (Hart 2013). Growing up in an atmosphere where there is separation, quarrels and abuse makes their health condition worse than a child in the same situation who grew in an environment filled with love and care from parents or caregiver. That's why the UK social care frowns at any family or parent who does not treat their children well or abuse them; they take the child away from you (Bowlby 2012).

This abuse could be:

- Emotional abuse
- Verbal abuse
- Financial abuse
- Sexual abuse

Sexual abuse:

Unfortunately, some couples or caregivers make love and show intimacy in front of their kids. Now, for me, that is sexual assault. That is exposing a child to what he or she is not supposed to know or forcefully introducing such act to a child.

Always tell your children to inform you if someone touches their private parts. It is better they grow and have sex than being abused by someone. At a certain age, show and tell them where their private parts are. They need to know. If you don't say, someone outside will help you do that which could be harmful.

Emotional abuse:

This type of ill treatment occurs where a child is disgraced or frightened consistently by his or her parent/caregiver. Emotional abuse is sometimes called psychological abuse because this emotional blackmail might affect the child psychologically as well as his/her development.

Verbal abuse:

Children can be said to have been abused verbally when a parent or caregiver speaks negatively, harshly and rudely to a child. The choice of words and response to conversations when training a child is important because that goes a long way to affect his or her behaviour in future.

Financial abuse:

Financial abuse has occurred when the money made available for the upkeep of the child is used for a personal purpose and not for the child's need, hence denying the child of the basic needs. The UK's social care sector is concerned about the way caregivers or parents handle their children, especially children with challenging behaviour (Bowlby 2012). One of the ways to help children with special needs is by effective communication given by the caregiver or parent (McLeod 2009). If there is no effective communication between such a child and parents, it might increase the level of frustration, aggression, self-harm, destructiveness and disruptiveness in the child's life. Children with special needs are not independent individuals. The majority of them have medical conditions, hence the reason they require particular attention from all caregivers especially their parents (McLeod 2009). Sometimes there might be conflicting ideas in the mind of both the medical personnel concerning the child and the parents. However, I think that the parent, especially the mum, knows exactly the development of the child, notwithstanding the medical ideas. That is why a child with learning difficulty needs the parents to help fill in the gap where nurses and doctors cannot fill. Children with disabilities whose parents are separated suffer a lot because they might end up getting random care from a father who has another woman and vice versa and sometimes might be forgotten because the mother or father might have their focus on the new family or relationship where they might have children as well. However, a child with disabilities whose parents are together find it easier to cope with the medical condition. Nurses and doctors play little role in their lives, and they get all the care and support from the family which makes it easier for their health to improve and this will enable inclusion in the society. The role parents play in lives of their kids cannot be overemphasised.

Ways to take care of children with special needs:

- Understanding their behaviour
- Follow guidelines for their medical personnel
- Open communication between their medical staff and parents
- Involving them in activities that will help promote their lives
- Show them love. However, let them know what is right and wrong by being firm when needed
- Improving their independence by encouraging them to do things you know that they can do
- Making the child's need paramount by focusing on whatever that will help the child medically, development and otherwise
- Respect their views unless it's to the detriment of their health or development
- Protect and respect their dignity if required
- Make confidentiality your watchword when dealing with them, especially their medical condition details, except with the necessary authority such as care workers, social workers or medical personnel
- Avoid sexual, verbal and financial abuse

When a child is forced to take part in sexual activities, the child is sexually abused. Often, children do not realise that what the abuser is teaching them is wrong until they are grown (NSPCC). For example, a five-year-old girl may not understand that she was abused until she becomes a teenager. Sexual assault, according to NSPCC, comes in two forms: contact abuse (where a child is raped or physically forced to take part in sexual activities) or non-contact form (where the child is made to watch her caregivers or parents make love). Sexual abuse occurs more in lives of children than we think and that's why the parent should explain sexual issues to children. Bad relationship and communication can make parents not realise what their child is going through or went through in the hands of the abuser. In this case, I would think that if the girl had a good relationship with her parents, she would have spoken out earlier or they would have noticed that there was something wrong with their child. The child should speak out because early intervention can help. Again, this depends on the level of relationship and closeness the child has with mum. Children from broken homes (divorced or separated couple) might be prone to this kind of issue more than kids from a happy couple. When parents are struggling in their relationships with their spouse or partner, it tends to affect their relationship with children which results in them not being aware of any abuse. More so, parents should not have sexual intercourse or do such acts before their children. Exposing kids to immoral acts can affect them later on in life.

Effects of sexual abuse on children in future:

- Self-harm
- Psychological effect
- Mental issues
- Lack of trust for family and friends
- Hatred for men or women
- Not wanting to have children in future
- Fear of the unknown
- Trauma
- Poor academic performance
- Poor relationships with others
- Change in personality
- Sexual abuse might change their sexual orientation

The roles of parents in the life of children

Many theories have proved that our relationship as a couple or partners goes a long way to affect our children's behaviour in the future and the society as a whole. For this scenario, we will focus on attachment theory. Bowlby posits that children have a certain level of attachment with their caregivers which could be the mother (from childhood). That is why every parent/caregiver, especially mothers, have a huge role to play in the lives of their child because their childhood experiences have a huge impact on their development and in their lives in future.

Attachment Theory

A person is said to be attached to another if there is a sense or feeling of security, closeness or bond between two people. When you smile to a child, and the child responds, reciprocity has occurred which is most times a two-way thing. Our behaviour to a child or relationship as caregivers goes a long way to affect them. How we handle our relationship with our spouses or partners goes a long way in shaping the children for the future, hence reciprocity influences the child's physical, societal and perceptive development.

It becomes the basis for the development of basic trust or mistrust and shapes how the child will relate to the world, learn, and form relationships throughout life (Simply Psychology). Therefore, you notice that children from broken homes have the tendency of having the mentality that separation is no big deal because their parents were separated. It shapes their ideology about marriage and relationship. Forming attachment with the child does not necessarily come from the person that changes the baby, it comes from the individual that communicates and responds to the child by playing and chatting with the baby. Therefore, responsiveness is the key to attachment. A child might not necessarily be attached to the mother.

A child can be attached to:

- Father
- Grandparents
- Caregiver
- Siblings
- Other relatives

For me, the importance of this theory is for us to sustain this attachment until they are old enough to take responsibility for their actions which is at the age of eighteen.

Advice for parents:

- Please pray for your children.
- Be nosy around them, especially when they are still young.
- Teach them to tell you if someone touches their private part, or even kiss them on the lips.
- Take every complaint they make serious and don't trivialise it.
- Listen to your child when she tells you stories because that will determine what he or she can tell you in future.
- Teach your child to speak out for themselves and don't keep her shut which could kill her self-confidence.
- Always remind them how beautiful or handsome they are so that they don't get too excited when someone tells them.
- Show them love always.
- Be careful who you leave them with or where they go.
- Male relatives or friends should not be allowed to stay with female children along, and vice versa.
- Check out for unnecessary closeness between father and child. Make sure your daughter realises that the father and daughter are different from husband and wife because some men abuse their daughters as well.

Advice for men:

- Do not pour out your sexual desire on a child.
- Be watchful who comes around your children.
- Don't be too close to your child as to want to make love to the person.
- Seek help secretly and in time if you notice you are developing feelings for your child at any point in time. This help could come from your spiritual leader (pastor), counsellor or GP.
- Be close to daughters but set your boundaries.

How can I support my child to fulfil their dreams

Promoting the rights of your children is paramount. A child has a right to fulfil their dreams irrespective of his or her physical abilities. It doesn't matter if the child needs special care or not. Every child for me has got a potential or a talent. The right of a child is actualised by channelling their mindset and lives towards their hobbies and likes. For me, a child is denied their human right if he or she is not encouraged or guided by the parents or caregivers to actualise their potentials. Helping your young ones to build his or her dreams or hobby is an important aspect of training a child and building a relationship. If you do not support the idea of your child, then it's hard for them to actualise their potentials. The first step in helping a child achieve his or her potential is by identifying what he or she likes to do. Some smart parents guides their child into a career they desire for them, thereby choosing their future or interest for them, the reason being that children learn fast at a young age and whatever you as a caregiver teach them becomes their dream and aspiration, hence the parents are the major determinant of their children's future. It is not a bad idea when parents choose a career path for a child, as long as he or she is guided into an area they feel comfortable.

Sometimes, such children grow into adults and decide to pursue a different career from what their parents taught them, thus the reason it's better to carefully identify what they love to do or let them exercise their rights by channelling their time and intelligence into their own chosen career. Another reason it's advisable to let them actualise their dreams is that if anything goes wrong in their career in future, the child might blame you. It's good to guide them into a good career, but I think it should be done based on their consent and out of their will to avoid denying them of their human rights as children.

Most parents and caregivers are scared of letting a child follow dreams such as music, dancing etc. Parents prefer their child to have a formal education and train to either become a doctor or a lawyer. Now, let me ask a question? If everyone becomes a professional doctor, who is going to entertain people through music, dance or football. Talents are gifts, qualities embedded in humans from God, so it should not be thrown away by leaving it for some other career. It is the duty of parents to discover their child's interest and guide them accordingly. Don't get me wrong, I will want my child to have a good standard of education, but I will also push him or her further in an area of interest.

However, there are so many factors that will hinder a parent from encouraging a child to achieve his or her potentials:

Too busy

Most parents or caregivers are too busy to realise the interest of their children. Parents could be busy with work, personal life or other activities.

Lack of resources

When there is not enough money to pursue your child's interest, it becomes an issue. Some talents such as singing or playing football might need you to pay for a child to gain more knowledge. Peradventure there is no money in your pocket; you can expose the child to listen to songs more or encourage the child to watch and play football at the field or garden. That way, they grow on their own pending when your circumstances change.

Fear of fame

Managing reputation can be difficult for children and young adults. Most parents may not want their children to go into modelling based on the fact that they do not want their children getting exposed to a particular lifestyle. Fame comes with its ups and down. If not managed properly, it might have an adverse effect on a child's advancement, but if it is handled correctly, both the child and their family will benefit from its proceeds.

Fear of associates

Some lines of career chosen by your children can expose them to friends or associates which might have both negative and positive impact on their lives.

Quest to gain formal education

Caregivers are of the opinion that when a child starts making money from either singing or other show business pursuits, they might lose interest in formal education. Again, I agree with that perception, but everything boils down on how you as a parent can manage the issue.

Fear of its impact on the child

When a child chooses to go into a career such as modelling, it's normal for most parents, especially from a religious background such as Christianity, to frown at the dress codes sometimes. It takes a mother to convince themselves that the mode of dressing or places such career path lead down will not have any adverse impact on their child. The fear of the negative consequences modelling will have on a child can affect the decision of the parents.

Location

Living in a remote area can either hinder a child from achieving their dreams or parents from actualising God's purpose for their lives. If you live a remote area, it might be difficult to access some facilities that can push up a child's dream.

See the following for tips that will enable you to manage your child through the hall of fame or stardom.

16 tips on how to support your child to actualise their dreams:

- Praying daily for the child. You can do that by praying for him or her during their shower. Sometimes, parents are so busy that they might not be able to pray for their children but I am sure all children get a shower daily or more depending on the environment and weather condition.
- Know your child's manager or coach.
- Know your child's friends and associates.
- Go to their shows depending on their chosen career.
- Be their friend.
- Listen to their questions.
- Ask them questions always.
- Find out the trend of the event in their lives so that you will know how to advise your child.
- Make your child know that you are proud of him or her. Always remind your child that he or she is handsome/beautiful, if you don't, someone else out there will do that for you.
- Show your children love by creating time to listen to their stories.
- Be ready to advise; remind them who they are and that they should comport themselves to maintain a good record for the future.
- Take them to activities that will teach them morals such as church and other educative programmes.
- Target what they watch. You can make out time and find out what kind of movies your children watch or decide to join them while watching. I know it can be difficult to achieve because most parents are busy with work and other things but I also know it is achievable if you put your heart to it.
- Using phones at night. Help your child manage his or her phone. For example, their phones should be turned off at a certain time of the evening as well as handed over to the parent. You obviously cannot control your child's entire life at a certain age, but you can try your best as a

- parent or caregiver until they get to adulthood.
- Minimise their accessibility to the internet especially at odd hours of the day.
- Forgiveness

Please be advised that forgiving your child if they have done wrong will enable you to keep track of their lives. Things might go wrong if you delay to forgive them and draw them back to yourself so that you can monitor what is going on in their lives. Pausing in silence when an issue arises in their lives can destroy a lot before you realise it.

Positive relationships: Introducing social Issues and how positive relationships can help solve problems.

Every bad thing we do is a social issue. The government tries daily to fight social problems. The problems usually start with the family. Social issues are those problems that occur in the society daily which is caused by people. For example, children who bully and mistreat other students have social problems (Campbell 2005). Parents should train their children in a way that will encourage the kids to free with them. When a child is free with the parents, it enables them to have an act of courage to tell their parents about some of the social issues they face in school or any social gathering. Most social problems start from how a child was brought up, but sometimes it's not the case.

Often, when there is a breach in communication between a child and parents, it affects the child's behaviour which in return brings issues with their friends and family. Giving your child a listening ear is a way to avoid your kids from getting involved in any social issues. Social problems in the society come into play amongst peers groups, friends and family. A scenario where a child goes to see the father and mother separately might affect the perception of the child about family and relationships. Children learn to be strong and independent from a base of loving and secure relationships with parents or caregivers (Ginsburg 2007). Leading causes of abuse are as a result unhealthy relationships that occur between parents or caregivers which in return has an adverse impact on the life of the child and behaviour in future (Danya Glaser, 2000). This causes a social problem either through the child going into crime, alcoholism, fighting or any other kind of social issues.

Personal, Social and Emotional Development (PSED) are three building blocks of future success in life (Roeser, Eccles, and Sameroff 2000). They are related to each other and often linked as one part of learning and development. A child's personal, social and emotional development must be managed effectively to avoid them getting involved in any form of social issues. To improve the well-being of children in certain areas and reduce inequalities between them, the Childcare Act 2006 places a duty on the local authorities (LAs) and their associates. Inclusive practice must be adopted which involves no discrimination against families or children and diversities of individuals and communities are valued and respected. Every child is unique, and their ability to learn is in them. The environment, people and schools go a long way to affect the development and behaviour of that given child (The National Strategies). Children should have experiences and support that will help them to develop a positive sense of themselves and others; respect for others; social skills; and a positive disposition to learn. Providers must ensure support for children's emotional well-being to help them to know themselves and what they can do (The National Strategies). If the relevant experiences are positive, the tendency that the child will contribute to the social problem of the society is small.

> **The following summarises the best approach to achieve a positive relationship with parents and individuals in the society:**
> - Form warm caring attachments with children in the groups.
> - Create useful relationships with parents, with everybody in the location and with caregivers.
> - Discover chances to give encouragement to children, with parents and caregivers acting as a role models who value differences and take account of different needs and expectations.
> - Plan for opportunities for children to play and learn, sometimes alone and in various groups.

Family

Family, the sole pride of an individual and the only shelter of a person, is a venerated system cherished across the globe. The caring mother, the kind father and the loving children contribute to the peace and prosperity of the family. These pillars strengthen the position and status of the family manifold by adding laughter, fun and comfort to the family. However, the illness or death of any family member immediately deteriorates the strong foundation of the family. Family health and well-being is necessary for its survival and sustenance. If your child is feeling sick, you will rush to a hospital to save them from any further illness. Similarly, the sickness of the parents forces the children to spend sleepless nights. It happens because the family shares the bond of great love for each other where health, well-being, fitness and strength are given paramount importance. The issues concerning the well-being of a family range from taking proper diets and doing simple daily exercises to taking proper sleep and adopting healthy lifestyles.

1. Eating healthy; Living healthy

When it comes to eating, we all rush to the snack shops to grab our favourite cakes, doughnuts, pizzas and burgers. Eating and enjoying the junk food has made the lives of our family vulnerable by bringing us to the brink of numerous illnesses. In the present day, the increased ratio of obesity, heart attacks, high blood pressure and increased cholesterol levels rise due to eating unhealthy food. The children, particularly fond of taking improper diet, are more prone to the fatal diseases than adults. To avoid the early life sickness, fatigue, stress and anxiety, a balanced diet is essential for all the members of a family. Many nutritionists and health practitioners advise the intake of eight glasses of water a day followed by the excessive use of green leafy vegetables and citrus fruits to lead a healthy and stable life.

2. Exercising for strength and stamina

A healthy body keeps a healthy mind while an unhealthy body creates troubles and problems. For this reason, a proper exercise is essential to build our stamina and to boost our strength. We must believe in the power of the daily push-ups, the planks, the muscle exercises and the pain-relieving activities to lead a happy, active and smart life. For this purpose, developing a habit of going to the gym or giving proper time to exercise at home should be made compulsory for every person in the family, particularly the young adults.

3. Sleeping for hours
Thanks to the 21st century gadgets, the cellular phones, the computers and the internet, our sleep patterns have taken a 360 degree turn. The maxim of early to bed and early to rise has now changed to late night rising and early morning sleeping. Today, every individual in the family spends long hours of the night on social media sites. Interestingly, the young generation of the modern era thinks that studying late at night results in good grades in the exams. On the contrary, psychologists prescribe at least six to eight hours of sleep daily for ensuring maximum health. Therefore, putting the children and yourself to bed at night contributes to the vigilance, activeness and smartness of the family.

4. Leading a healthy lifestyle

We all must avoid the phrase 'My life; my choice' if we want to remain healthy, happy and contented. Adopting a good lifestyle is the answer to all the worries, issues and problems relating to health and well-being of the family. Learn to spend less, eat less, sleep more and work more to avoid the later life health issues and concerns. The individuals who do not lead a planned life are more likely to suffer from stress, fatigue and anxiety in life as compared to those who follow a proper pattern in life. It is advisable to inculcate the effective habits and good manners in the young generation to make them healthy, active, intelligent and useful individuals. Health and well-being, the two parameters of success, are necessary for leading a worth remembering and worth following life. The parents and the children in the family should ensure their health, safety and security in all aspects of life. The health of a family can only be gained, restored and reclaimed if, and only if, the family members work together to contribute to their well-being, happiness and peace.

Who is the most stubborn person in the family?

Anyone can be stubborn, so I would not categorically say that stubbornness is a word attached to either a mother, child or father. I think it's best to be stubborn or be a strong-willed person but in a right way. Do not be stubborn over trivial things that are of no societal, environment or spiritual use to you and family. Before you become obstinate about something or a decision, evaluate it properly and have a think about all decisions and advice you have received and make your conclusion based on your findings. You do not want to make a grievous and unforgettable mistake in life and your family, all in the name of being that 'stubborn in quote' individual. Your ability to make an adjustment and see reason with others for me is wisdom, however don't live in people's opinion and views because it sometimes causes more harm than good.

Ways a stubborn attribute can be used to achieve greatness:

- Stubborn individuals can be great leaders because a leader should not be influenced by his subjects. Listening to the team can be an excellent idea but a scenario where everyone controls you as a leader, and you cannot stand firm on your decisions.
- Individuals that are stubborn can be nicest people if understood.
- Those that are stubborn can have the heart to help others in most cases but not all cases.
- Stubborn people might just lack love in their lives and

feel they do not get appreciated enough for sacrifices they make. Rather, people tend to focus on their bad attribute which, of course, everyone has.
- Such individuals that can speak on behalf of others to achieve a fight or a common goal
- People that say things the way they are without pretending or mincing words are also stubborn in nature.
- A stubborn person usually is not double-sided. With them, what you see is what you get.
- Stubborn people usually feel remorseful and find easy to forgive people when they wrong them.
- Such individual makes sacrifices for family and friends. They go out of their way to do things for others and worry a lot about others as well.

How you can handle a stubborn family member:

- Show them love.
- Listen to their opinion.
- Be patient with them.
- Try to solve their complaints from the root to avoid reoccurrence.
- Identify the triggers for their stubbornness.
- Do not be quick to blame them for anything because that makes it worse.
- Come down to their level and flow with their complaints.
- Speak to them nicely about their attribute when they are in the best state of mind.
- Try not to blame all the time because they cannot be wrong always.
- Tell them the truth but identify what the other has done wrong if applicable so that they don't feel like a victim or marginalised.

Major purpose of family: extended family and their ill treatment to their wives.

The immediate family consist of father, mother and children. Other relatives of the family will include cousins, sisters, brothers, aunties and uncles. Unity is what joins this family together, but unfortunately, the reverse is the case most times. A woman (wedded wife) has a lot to contend with once married into a home. Trying to cause issues between your brothers and his wife is a wrong approach in changing any woman - that is, if she is a bad person. The dialogue between parents or heads of the family can help tackle any issue rather than gossips, slanders, unnecessary fights and quarrels. The society will never advise taking the law into your hands, neither will the Bible (for Christians). Rather, the community will prefer the court to handle any conflict (Judge) as well as letting God be the judge for Christians. If you apply this rule to the family with your brother's wife, you will find out that you fight with her less. All you need to do is to pray about the issues you noticed as well as speak to your parents and brother so that they can know how best to handle the issues. Unfortunately, sometimes the man's father and mother might be the problem, making it difficult for conflict resolution. Be that as it may, be careful not to fight your brother's wife because whatever you do might come back to you.

Purpose of a family

The community consists of different families. When a family stays together, it has a positive impact on the society and the world as a whole. Every good business, organisation and group starts from a real family. The purpose of a family is to work together to pull through challenges that come in life and to achieve certain objectives such as happiness, peace, stability, children and much more.

Qualities of a good family:

- Peace
- Communication

- Family that respects God and the society
- Welcoming
- Watches each other's back
- United
- Upholds the truth
- Frowns at wrong
- No fights
- Responsible
- Willingness to reconcile

The way you carry your wife is the way your family or relative takes her. Some make life very simple including their lives and everything around it. Men who possess such good attribute do not suspect their wives, they are not over possessive and do not bother about their phones and who speaks to them. Also, they do not hold a grudge; they forgive because they live for the moment. However, they should strike a balance between respecting their wives and their pure nature. Women that are married to men with such attribute sometimes wonder if their spouse loves them.

Reasons in-laws hate the wives:

- Jealousy
- Feeling of diverted love
- Feeling that all their brother's wealth goes to the wife's family
- Greed
- They want to be in control of their brother's marriage
- Fear that their brother might neglect their need

Best ways women can handle such family:

- Know when to speak
- Do not wish them bad
- Show them love as you would show to your people
- Be patient in such matters
- Reduce contact with them to avoid more issues

- Do not complain about everything; carefully choose issues that matter

Lessons for men:

- Always stand up for her when she is right and correct her when she is wrong
- Do not let your family override her or disrespect her
- Respect her always
- Give her listening ears, come down to her level and look to her complaints. Do not trivialise it but rather give her good advice and make her feel happy
- Always tell her how much you love her and how beautiful she is
- Love your family but do not let anyone disrespect or come in between your wife and children

How to maintain a peaceful and healthy family:

- Spending time together
- Praying
- Having an awareness that you all are one
- Tolerating one another
- Correcting in love
- Acknowledge the rough times
- Support each other emotionally, materially and otherwise
- Do not castigate yourselves outside
- Be ready to defend your family as and when necessary
- Creating a balance between a chosen career and family
- Love and admire one another's achievement and looks
- Be flexible enough to accept changes
- Make communication your watchword

A family is made up of a father, mother and child and it is one of the most important aspects of our lives. A family has the capacity to make you or mar you. For example, someone might or might not want to marry into a family because it either has a good name or a bad reputation in the community. The head of the family is the man from the societal perspective and also biblically, God made the (men) fathers the head of homes and families. It doesn't mean that the women do not play a role in families. In fact, women play more multitasking roles than men in families but they are there to help men maintain and sustain the family by taking care of the children, grannies, meals and other aspects that define a family. For children and children in need, the family is the bedrock of their future, hence the reason the Bible encourage you to train up your child well (Proverbs 22:6) and in schools, the government encourages a high standard of moral for their future. Furthermore, for the older people, the family determines how happy they will be at end of the day especially when they have reached the age of eighty and above. While the family helps mould the behaviour and future of the children through love and support which are given by parents and relatives, it consequently affects their lives and relationship with others.

Coming to the older folk who may have spent most of their years having fun and working, you will realise that individuals that put in hard work to sustain their homes enjoy more. These older folks have their family members such as daughters, sons, grandchildren and great-grandchildren coming around to visit as often as possible. This visit increases their number of years on earth and they look forward to living many more years ahead, whereas the folks that do not have family tend to feel lonely at that point; their spouse, partner or friends might not be alive to keep them company. No one will judge you if you do not have children due to health reasons and personal decision. I am aware that creating a home is an area every young adult should venture into because it will help you in future, if you put in your best through the word of God and obeying the rules that govern your community.

Reasons people avoid having families:

- Fear of responsibility
- No money to take care of them
- Not finding the right spouse
- Fear of childbirth for the women
- Fear of having a change in looks and shape

- Not ready to commit to a relationship
- Health issues such as low sperm count, fibroid, no womb and other health-related issues
- They came from the wrong family
- They were abused by their family
- Fear of their negative past experience
- Some people are married to individuals that do not want kids so they are forced not create a family

Reasons you should create a family:

- For companionship at old age
- To maintain your family name
- Someone gave birth to you, it's wise to do the same
- Feel the joy of parenthood
- You will look back and be proud of yourself
- Fun to see a mini-you
- For Christmas Seasons- you spend Christmas with family and friends
- To contribute to the community because if everyone decides not have babies/ families, then in the next couple of years we will not have a community or society

I am encouraging you to create a family if you can because the Bible values families; and the society places strong value on families and healthy relationship. Create one and enjoy it. Although, it's not built in one day, it's a journey that is worth the stress. Ultimately, you will reap the fruit of your labour at old age.

CONCLUSION

It has been proved that 90% causes of poor health, especially in married women, is a result of loneliness and sadness caused by unhealthy relationship in their homes. Many couples are lonely and sad in their homes, more than some singles. It feels like they are kept in a box with no space to breath just because we are experimenting with each other. We do not want to make an effort to find out what our spouse expects of us and how they want to be loved because what you perceive as love is different from how another might want to be loved. Do you want a marriage full of peace and achievements? If yes, make up your mind to stay in your home and enjoy it, not endure. I do not want you to be in your marriage solely because of your children, family name, business benefits, religious beliefs etc. I want you to remain there because you love, cherish and value your home, and the happiness you derive from there is immeasurable.

'Remember, nothing worth's your happiness as said in the bible nothings is as good as merry heart'
Proverbs 17:22

I am yet to see that couple that does not disagree. However, it depends on how you manage each other's excesses and how much time you are willing to invest to make your relationship last in happiness and with passion. Seek to learn or master the skills peculiar to your home because that will enable you to sustain it and live in peace and harmony rather than endure all your life in order to stay married. Invite Jesus into your home and He will give you wisdom, and knowledge on how best to maintain your home will roll into your mind daily. However, before you invite him, be advised that you need to develop a good relationship with him by firstly making him your Lord and saviour through his word and prayer. Then, he will start giving your personal ideas on how to manage your affairs in conjunction with the insight you have derived from reading this book. My life is a living example because my marriage was edge of crumbling sometime in year 2017 with so many issues I never imagined I could go through. Whether you are a leader in the church or a pastor, if you do not officially invite him to take over the affairs in your home, then you will struggle to maintain relevance. Make that decision today and I am certain Jesus will turn up for you, just like he did in my life and relationship.

Shareable quote idea for you:

The essence of life is to live it, enjoy it and have a positive impact on others so live it, enjoy it and impact into others
~Ngozi Emele~

REFERENCES/RECOMMENDATIONS

Books:
- Allan. Dr. Corey, *Naked Marriage*, Simple Marriage (2016)
- Berk, Laura E., *Child Development*, Pearson International Edition (2005)
- Bowlby, John, *A Secure Base: Clinical Application of Attachment Theory*, Routledge (1995)
- Bowly, John, *Attachment: Volume One of the Attachment and Loss Trilogy: Attachment Vol 1 (Attachment & Loss)*, Pimlico (1997)
- Dorman, Marianne, *Praying*
- Hart, Roger A., *Children's Participation*, Routledge (1997)

Studies and papers:
- Ainsworth. M. D. S., & Bell S. M. (1970). Attachment, Exploration and Separations. Illustrated by the behaviour of a one-year-olds in strange situation. *Child Development* 41, 49-67.
- Campbell, Marilyn A (2005), Cyber bullying: An old problem in a new guise?, *Australian Journal of Guidance and Counselling* 15(1):68-76.
- Dollard, J., & Miller, N. E. (1950). Personality and Psychotherapy: An Analysis in Terms of Learning, Thinking, and Culture. New York: McGraw-Hill.
- Ginsburg, Kenneth R. (2007), The Importance of Play in Promoting Healthy Child Development and Maintaining Strong Parent-Child Bonds, *Pediatrics*, January 2007, Volume 119 / Issue 1
- Glaser, Danya (2000), Child abuse and neglect and the brain--a review, *J Child Psychol Psychiatry*. 2000 Jan;41(1):97-116.
- Richter, Dr. Linda, The importance of caregiver-child interactions for the survival and healthy development of young children: a review, *World Health Organization* (2004)

- Roeser, Robert W., Eccles, Jacquelynne S., Sameroff, Arnold J. (2000), School as a Context of Early Adolescents' Academic and Social-Emotional Development: A Summary of Research Findings, *The Elementary School Journal*, Vol. 100, No. 5, Special Issue: Non-Subject-Matter Outcomes of Schooling [II] (May, 2000), pp. 443-471

Other helpful resources:
- 8 Reasons NOT To Cut Your Baby's Umbilical Cord by Kelly Winder, Updated: January 30, 2016, https://www.bellybelly.com.au/birth/reasons-not-to-cut-your-babys-umbilical-cord/
- Baby Centre
- Bible Study Tool
- Emergency home birth: https://www.babycentre.co.uk/a557710/emergency-home-birth
- Emergency Labor: What to Do If You Have to Give Birth Alone: https://www.whattoexpect.com/pregnancy/emergency-labor
- Les Brown, *The Power of a Positive Mindset*, YouTube
- McLeod, S. A (2009). Attachment theory. Retrieved from Simply Psychology: https://www.simplypsychology.org/attachment.html
- The National Strategies, Early Years
- NSPCC
- Romance Free Dictionary by Farlex
- Sexual abuse Legislation, policy, and guidance by NSPCC
- SimplyPsychology.org